NAVAJO JEWELRY

A Legacy of Silver and Stone

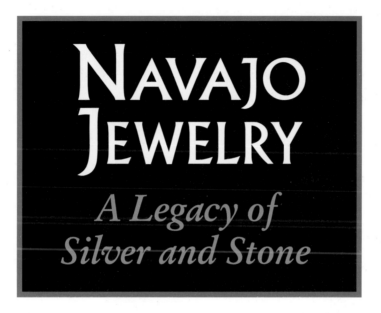

NAVAJO JEWELRY

A Legacy of Silver and Stone

by Lois Essary Jacka
Photographs by Jerry Jacka

NORTHLAND PUBLISHING

The text type was set in Stempel Garamond
The display type was set in Albertus
Designed by Julie Sullivan, Sullivan Scully Design Group
Cover design and Art Direction by Trina Stahl
Edited by Erin Murphy and Stephanie Bucholz
Production Supervised by Lisa Brownfield
Composed in the United States of America

Manufactured in Hong Kong by Sing Cheong Printing Co. Ltd.

First Impression 1995
Second Printing, 1996
ISBN 0-87358-609-3
Library of Congress Catalog Card Number 95-16911

Cataloging-in-Publication Data
Jacka, Lois Essary.
    Navajo jewelry : a legacy of silver and stone / by Lois Essary Jacka. — 1st ed.
        p.   cm.
    Includes bibliographical references and index.
    ISBN 0-87358-609-3 (sc)
    1. Navajo Indians—Jewelry. I. Title.
E99.N3J26 1995   95-16911
739.27'089'972—dc20

0638/7.5M/10-96

Cover: The Mittens of Monument Valley in Navajo Country and finely crafted jewelry by Mary Marie Yazzie. The squash blossom necklace is set with Royston turquoise; the bracelet with Morenci.
Photo on page 5 by Ben Wittick, courtesy School of American Research Collections in the Museum of New Mexico, neg. no. 15713. Frontispiece: Contemporary silver jewelry set with Chinese turquoise by Thomas Singer.

For our moms, Rose and Rowena;
our kids, Cindy, Mike, and Kathy;
and our grandkids, Dan and Sally
(the one who wanted to know why the last
book wasn't dedicated to the family).

In memory of Lovena Ohl,
a guiding light for Native American artists,
and Herbert Taylor (1951–1996).
We deeply regret that the world has lost
a great Navajo artist but, even more,
we mourn the loss of a dear friend.

CONTENTS

OPPOSITE: *Thomas Curtis, Sr., excels at a distinctive style of silverwork. A versatile artist, he fashions silver into many forms including containers, flatware, and traditional jewelry. The primary techniques used in these pieces are fabrication, stamp and chisel work, and repoussé.*

IN THE BEGINNING

ABOVE: *James Little created this Monument Valley scene in 18-karat gold with a moon symbol against a lapis lazuli sky. Stars are formed by the natural matrix of the stone and are represented by the crosses on the chains. The lost wax technique was used in making this necklace.*

IN THE BEGINNING

The Southwestern United States is noted for its unique beauty, but one particular region stands out above all others: the only place where four states— Arizona, New Mexico, Utah, and Colorado—intersect. This site, known as the "Four Corners," is a desolate spot, but radiating out from that hub like the spokes of a wheel is a region, with ambiguous boundaries, that encompasses parts of all four states. Rich in history, this is a dramatic land, mysterious and alluring, that awes by its sheer magnitude.

Within the heart of this area lies the Navajo Nation, the ancestral homeland of some two hundred thousand *Diné,* the People, the name preferred by many Navajos. Their reservation of some sixteen million acres sprawls across the vast reaches of northeastern Arizona and north-western New Mexico and nips up into southern Utah. It includes pine-forested mountain ranges, red rock canyons, desert rivers, rugged juniper-covered hillsides, still lakes and rushing mountain streams, grass-covered rangelands, and giant monoliths and pinnacles rising abruptly from barren stretches of high plateau country.

It is a land of beauty that mesmerizes with its intensity, colors, shapes, textures, and designs.

It is a still, silent land that whispers of timelessness—a place where the remnants of ancient civilizations stand serenely under azure skies awaiting yet another day.

It is a spiritual land that touches the soul; to the Navajo it is a holy land guarded by sacred mountains in each of the Four

Directions: Blanca Peak, east; Mount Taylor, south; San Francisco Peaks, west; and Mount Hesperus, north.

The Navajos are descendants of Athapascan groups who migrated from southwestern Canada and Alaska. This was not a concentrated effort to forge a route; small groups simply traveled south and eastward, camping, hunting, and foraging for food, remaining in one place as long as their needs were met.

Individual bands approached the Southwest separately from different directions over a long period of time. Each group brought various traditions acquired during journeys that lasted for generations.

Because they were a nomadic people who built few, if any, permanent shelters and made little pottery, evidence of early occupation is sketchy at best. Differing theories place their arrival at anytime from the fourth to the thirteenth century.

Through the years, the ancestors of the Athapascans became separated into two groups. One branch began roaming farther

BELOW: *Jesse Monongye's belt buckle, titled "The New Beginning," features snow-capped mountains of lapis lazuli and dolomite (white). The North Star (upper left corner) reigns over a star-studded night sky; an abstract sun face appears at upper right. Above an opal moon, the Big Dipper is made of turquoise. A shooting star streaks downward toward a rainbow of colors that represent the coming of dawn. "My grandmother said that as the earth rotates, there is a sunset and sunrise every moment of every day," Jesse said. "There is always a new beginning—somewhere. The rainbow colors at dawn tell us of a change in the season or the weather."*

south and the other gravitated westward. The former would become the Apaches, the latter the Navajos.

Records from Francisco Vásquez de Coronado's Spanish expedition of 1540 made no mention of encountering the Navajos. In fact, the first historical reference to the People was in a Franciscan missionary's report of 1626. Father Zarate-Salmeron briefly commented that the "Apache de Navahu" (Strangers of the Cultivated Fields) lived "somewhere in the hinterlands."

In the meantime, however, Don Juan de Oñate had entered New Mexico in 1598, bringing with him some four hundred people—soldiers, priests, and settlers with their households. Appointed Governor and Captain General, Oñate's task was to distribute land to the colonists and bring the Pueblos into submission. Those who didn't agree to pay homage to the King of Spain and the Christian God were subjected to brief, bloody battles that they were destined to lose.

Although a successful revolt was staged by the Pueblos in 1680, it was a short-lived victory. Twelve years later the Spaniards returned in force, crushing all opposition as they came. Some Pueblos escaped and joined the Navajos, but hundreds were captured and sold into slavery in the West Indies; the rest lived under the rule of the conquering Spaniards.

By the 1700s the Navajos were well established in the area, where they lived in forked-stick hogans (the old triangular-shaped dwellings that were the forerunner of the dome-roofed, hexagonal log dwellings adopted later). They hunted for game, raided other tribes, and cultivated their own fields. Noted for their adaptability and quick-wittedness, they had adopted the farming methods of their Pueblo neighbors.

Navajo Indians

The Navajos were affected much less negatively by the presence of the Spaniards than were the Pueblos, who were ruled with an iron hand. Raids against the Spanish provided the Navajos with iron objects, silver ornaments and, more importantly, livestock. With sheep to provide wool and Pueblo refugees to serve as tutors, Navajo women soon became expert weavers, for which they would become noted.

The Indian population of the Southwest increased rapidly, and the entire territory soon became crowded. To the south were the Apaches; to the north, the Utes; to the northeast, the Comanches; to the east and southeast, the Pueblos. Intermingled among the Pueblo villages and on outlying ranches were the Spaniards and New Mexican settlers. The Navajos began spreading farther westward toward their present reservation homeland.

In 1842, Mexico gained independence from Spain and the Spanish soldiers departed. This offered a golden opportunity to the wealthy and powerful Navajos. Crops were plentiful, herds were large, and there were horses to ride on forays against enemy Indian tribes and the Mexicans who were engaged in trying to build a new government. Continuing raids produced more livestock, captives who were kept as servants or sold into slavery, and coveted Spanish and Mexican silverwork. Navajo clothing was decorated with rows of silver buttons, and silverwork adorned their bridles. Christened the "Lords of the Soil" by the New Mexicans, the Navajos continued to thrive.

It was too good to last. Return raids by the Utes, Apaches, and Comanches plagued the Navajos; even the normally peaceful Pueblos and the New Mexicans sometimes rode against them. A culture clash between New Mexican citizens and the rapidly growing American population caused further conflict. No one was safe and ranches were rapidly being abandoned.

When the U.S. declared war on Mexico in 1846, the Americans took Santa Fe with little resistance. A time of utter chaos followed. Treaties between the Americans and Navajos were continually made and broken. The Navajos still lived in small bands, and the Americans could not understand that no one "chief" had the authority to sign a treaty for the entire Navajo population.

The Navajos also had legitimate complaints. They were being pushed ever-farther westward by the encroachment of New Mexican ranchers and American settlers, and they faced constant raids. Their livestock and goods were plundered; their people were taken captive and shipped into Mexico as slaves. Meetings and attempts at reconciliation ended unsatisfactorily for both sides. As the situation worsened, American troops moved into Fort Defiance, deep in Navajo country.

Still, the Americans could not gain control of the Diné. When a detachment was sent to find a band of Navajos, the Navajos simply "disappeared" into some remote canyon or the rugged terrain of some mountain range, driving their livestock before them. There, they hid out until the soldiers gave up and went elsewhere.

With the advent of the Civil War, the soldiers left Fort Defiance for the southern battlefield, and the entire countryside became a maelstrom of violence, totally out of control. Comanches, Apaches, Navajos, Utes, Pueblos, and white outlaws rode rampant, and New Mexican citizens fought for their lives.

However, with the arrival of Colonel Christopher "Kit" Carson in 1863, the world as the Navajo knew it was about to come to an end. When the Navajos refused to surrender, Carson turned neighboring tribes into "bounty hunters"; not only did he pay some of them to fight the Navajos, but he offered rewards of twenty dollars for each captured horse or mule, one dollar for each captured sheep.

It was guerrilla warfare at its best—or worst. The Lords of the Soil were the underdogs now. Under the auspices of the government and without fear of reprisal, everyone rode against the Diné, claiming livestock, women, and children as spoils of war. Crops could no longer be tended, herds were rapidly depleted, and no trail was safe from invaders.

As the Navajos moved ever farther into the mountains and canyons, Colonel Carson set out to destroy their way of life. Swooping across the countryside, the Americans left a trail of destruction: Livestock was captured, hogans were set ablaze, fruit trees were chopped down, crops were confiscated, and fields were trampled and burned.

Some Navajos took refuge among the Havasupais, Apaches, and Pueblos. Others escaped into the Grand Canyon and the rugged arroyos along the Little Colorado River, or they fled northward to Navajo Mountain or across the San Juan River.

A January 1864 raid against the Navajos in Canyon de Chelly was the beginning of the end. Left with no food or shelter, the Navajos had only one hope of survival: surrender. Starving Diné by the thousands began crowding into Fort Defiance, where they were given small rations of food.

On March 6, 1864, the first twenty-four hundred Navajos left for Fort Sumner on the "Long Walk"—a tragic walk of over three hundred miles that will always be remembered by the Diné. Stragglers were often killed or captured by enemy tribes, New Mexicans, or Americans; the People were ravaged by illness, hunger, and homesickness. They were not only leaving their homeland but, when they passed Mount Taylor in New Mexico, they were no longer within the protective circle of the Four Sacred Mountains. They were leaving hallowed ground—their ceremonies would no longer be effective; the deities would not hear their prayers.

The Navajos were accustomed to mountains and canyons, but soon only vast desolate plains stretched before them endlessly. Little did they know that things would get worse once they arrived at their destination.

Fort Sumner (called *Hwéeldi* by the Navajos, *Bosque Redondo* by the New Mexicans) became "home" to over eight thousand Navajos, but it was estimated that at least that many slipped away before the surrender. Those who reached the fort were turned out onto forty square miles of flat, barren land with no shelters. Shallow pits covered with branches or hides served as sleeping quarters for most; the women cooked on open fires outside.

Four long years of deprivation followed. The crops planted by the Diné failed due to poor farming conditions and natural disasters: caterpillars, flooding, hail, drought, and wind. The wood was soon used up, the alkaline water from the Pecos River made the Navajos ill, and many were reduced to eating rodents and wild roots.

For a time, the ever-ingenious Navajos found a way to secure additional supplies. Cardboard ration tickets, which were used to obtain food supplies, were distributed among the Navajos as they passed through a gate into a corral. They quickly learned to forge the tickets and, when the government substituted stamped metal ration tickets, those were also forged.

A few Navajos had learned to work metal prior to their arrival at Bosque Redondo and others apparently learned while there. These men were undoubtedly responsible for at least some of the forgeries. It was reported that at one time as many as three thousand extra tickets were being passed around. The army finally sent to Washington for elaborate metal disks that could not be copied.

In *The Navajo,* Ruth Underhill suggests, "When we look for the origin of silverwork, perhaps this craft [the forgeries], developed under stress of hunger, may point to an early inspiration."

It may have been inspirational, but it did little to abate hunger, and conditions continued to worsen. Poisonous weeds killed the sheep, and Ute and Comanche raiding parties swept down to steal livestock and kidnap Navajo women and children who were then sold into slavery. Hundreds of Navajos died and others escaped, but most of those who did were killed or captured by enemy tribes, New Mexicans, or the military.

The ill-advised plan to turn the Navajos into peaceful citizens had reached an impasse. They could not support themselves at Bosque Redondo and, despite the millions funded for provisions, conditions were deplorable. Greed and graft ran rampant among the politicians, agents, and others responsible for supplying the fort. Debate raged in Washington for years before it was decided to transfer the Diné to an Oklahoma reservation. The desperate Navajos made one final plea to be allowed to return to the mesas and redrock canyons of their homeland. At last, the government agreed—if the Navajos would sign a new treaty.

After four long years of tribulation, they were willing to sign anything. Twenty-nine headmen put their mark on the "Old Paper" (as it is known today) and, on June 18, 1868, the People began their homeward journey with probably two thousand fewer than had arrived four years earlier. However, their newly designated reservation did not include all of their old territory, and it had been laid to waste by the Americans. Many more years of hardship would follow before the People could rebuild their lives.

TOP: *Standing Rock near Salina Springs, Arizona.*

BOTTOM: *Brass bracelets, such as this one from the late 1860s (lower right), were among the first jewelry items made by Navajo smiths. The stamped conchas are from a belt, circa 1870; the late 1880s squash blossom necklace belonged to Hoskininnii, a well-known Navajo leader in the Monument Valley area. The silver-plated belt buckle (upper right) was made from Santa Fe Railroad brakemen's badges, probably in the 1920s or early 30s.*

THE ORIGIN
OF AN ART

THE ORIGIN OF AN ART

Prior to the coming of the Spaniards, the Native Americans of the Southwest had no metal or livestock. The Navajos were undoubtedly envious of the strange new enemies who rode horses and had guns, bridle bits, tools, even silver-decorated bridles and saddles. And, even though many of these items were procured through raids, the Diné must have wished for a steady and reliable source.

Learning metalsmithing, however, would have required tools and materials the Navajos did not have, and the Spaniards were sworn enemies. Contact was far too brief to allow even the quick-learning Diné to acquire Spanish skills.

At what time the Navajos actually learned to work metal is debatable. Some say it happened before the Long Walk, while others differ, but it is generally accepted that one of the first blacksmiths was Atsidi Sani (Old Smith), or Herrera Delgadito (Little Slim Ironworker), as he was known by the Mexicans. Margery Bedinger states in *Indian Silver* that "In about 1850 [Atsidi Sani] journeyed south to a Mexican settlement near Mount Taylor... and persuaded one of the inhabitants, Nakai Tsosi (Thin Mexican), to teach him how to form the black metal."

If not the first Navajo blacksmith, Atsidi Sani was the most prominent, and probably the most proficient, of that era. Noted for making knives and bridle bits, he would teach his craft to many Navajos, including some of the men at Bosque Redondo.

Most of the early metalwork was utilitarian, but buttons, rings, earrings, belt pieces strung on leather, and a few bridle ornaments were also made. Multiple bracelets of twisted metal were often worn on one arm; others, hammered out of copper or brass, had lightly scratched, simple designs.

Navajos had worn silver ornaments and sported silver bridle decoration for at least fifty years, but those articles were of Spanish origin, either traded or stolen from Mexicans, or taken as spoils of war from Utes or Comanches.

In 1853 (eleven years prior to incarceration at Bosque Redondo), Indian Agent Henry Dodge moved into a newly built stone house near Fort Defiance, made friends with the Navajos, and eventually married a Navajo woman. It is also reported that he brought along a blacksmith and a Mexican silversmith.

Many years later, the agent's aged son, Chee Dodge, would say that "Old Smith [Atsidi Sani] came to the agency to look on and learned some things." The supposition is that Atsidi Sani learned or perhaps improved his skills by watching these men, but whether his skills included silverwork is unknown. Those years were particularly chaotic; raiding and clashes with other tribes were at their height. Therefore, the times were not particularly conducive to learning a new craft, and silver would have been difficult to obtain.

Atsidi Sani's great-nephew, Grey Moustache, is quoted as saying, "It was not until the Navajo came back [from Bosque Redondo] that he [Atsidi Sani] learned to make silver jewelry." And Chee Dodge would add that "The Navajo didn't make any silver of their own while they were at Fort Sumner. How could they? They were locked up there like sheep in a corral. They had only a very little silver in those days, which they bought from the Mexicans."

Several newspaper articles published in New Mexico during those years made claims of Navajo silverwork. "Navajos at Fort Sumner are skilled enough to make good bridle bits and other articles of horse equipage in iron and silver," one reported. "Amongst the chiefs now on this reservation, many are dressed in comfortable and even elegant style, in black cloth and buckskin, well-fitted to their bodies and ornamented with silver buttons of their own execution and design."

The silver buttons were most assuredly not of Navajo design; they had been procured from Mexicans for years. Furthermore, this entire account seems doubtful considering the deplorable state of Navajo life during exile. One might suspect that the editors, possibly influenced by corrupt politicians who were noted for their greed-and-graft mentality, were trying to make living conditions appear much better than they were.

Historic photographs show the Bosque Redondo Navajos poorly dressed in cotton clothing or wrapped in blankets against the bitter cold. It is unlikely that even "the chiefs" mentioned in the newspaper article would have dressed as described. If any did, they must have been the exception, and any silver ornaments they possessed were probably trade goods. It seems much more probable that the Navajos learned to work silver soon after they resettled in their homeland.

Atsidi Sani is generally considered the founder of the silver craft, but whether he learned it from the same Mexican who taught him metalwork or from another Mexican friend is unconfirmed. However, his first students were his four sons who, in turn, taught others.

With peaceful conditions, Mexican smiths began traveling onto the reservation to trade their silver for Navajo livestock.

As the silversmith fashioned a piece, the Navajo who ordered
it would certainly have observed and perhaps even assisted by
working the bellows. Considering their propensity for acquir-
ing new skills easily, the Navajos must have recognized this as
an excellent opportunity to learn to craft their own silver ornaments. It has been recorded that they were casting jewelry as
early as 1870.

Silver coins, acquired from soldiers at Fort Defiance and
Fort Wingate, were melted down, then poured into hand-carved
molds to create a particular design or a simple ingot, which was
then cooled, hammered into a thin sheet of silver, and trimmed
to the proper shape.

The learning process, however, was still gaining momentum.
In 1884 John Lorenzo Hubbell (the much-admired Don
Lorenzo of Hubbell Trading Post at Ganado) and his partner,
C. N. Cotton, hired Mexican smiths to teach silversmithing to
the Navajos, and began furnishing some of the coins used to
fashion the silver ornaments. The first Navajo silverwork was
rather crude and quite heavy, but it showed a lot of promise.
Designs were symmetrical even though smiths had no precision
implements; in fact, they had few tools of any kind, often just a
hammer, some files, and scissors or metal snips.

Washington Matthews, a young army surgeon from Fort
Wingate and the most noted Navajo authority of the 1880s,
recorded the tools and techniques used by Navajo smiths.
For anvils they acquired pieces of train rail, kingpins from
wagons, any old pieces of iron large enough, hard stones, or
tree stumps.

Forges were made of mud or sandstone, the bellows from
goatskin bags, and crucibles from anything that worked—

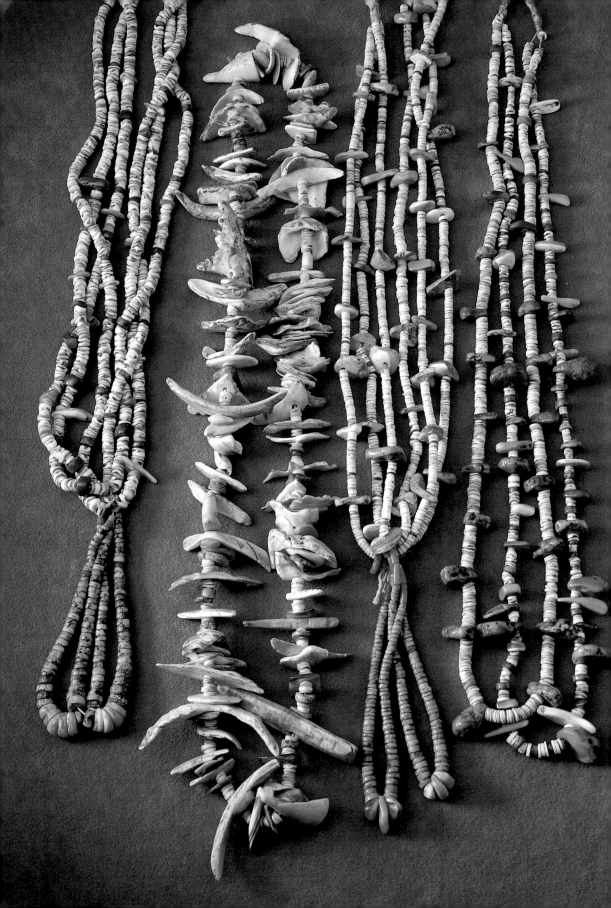

stones with small hollows, tumbler-sized pottery pieces made especially for that purpose, or iron pipes with one end flattened, turned up, and sealed.

A semicircle or V-shaped groove was sometimes cut into anvils for shaping bracelets; the first molds were made from baked clay and discarded after a time. Later molds were carved from iron, wood, or soft sandstone, which was greased with mutton tallow to prevent sticking.

Some of the first silver items made by Navajo smiths were the buttons they had previously obtained from Mexicans. Men's trousers, jackets, leather pouches, bridles, saddles, gun scabbards, *ketohs,* or bow guards, the wide leather bands worn on the left wrist to protect from the bowstring's recoil, and belts were adorned with these silver ornaments. They also decorated the moccasins and leggings of both sexes, and women's blouses had rows of them at the neck, across the shoulder, down the front, and running the length of both sleeves.

Many bracelets were nothing more than narrow bands with notches cut on either side; others were made of twisted wire or plain silver with simple designs scratched in with a file. Conchas for belts were decorated with scalloped edges, punched holes, and incised and stamped designs. Rings were simple decorated bands of silver; earrings were large loops that passed through pierced ears. Silver replaced the tin decorations on ketohs.

LEFT: *This* ketoh *(c. 1920s or 30s) is decorated with silver wire, repoussé designs, turquoise, and silver buttons. Procured from Mexicans for many years, buttons were probably one of the first silver items made by Navajo smiths.*

OPPOSITE: *These shell and turquoise Navajo necklaces, from the 1920s and 30s, are the forerunners of the turquoise nugget necklaces that are popular among the Navajo today.*

ABOVE: *Navajo* ketohs *or bow guards. The three pieces at left were made during the late 1800s. All are decorated with stamped designs; the one at the top includes repoussé. The cast* ketoh *(lower right) dates between 1900 and 1915, the two with turquoise settings from the 1930s.*

RIGHT: *Navajo concha belt of the early 1900s. Decorative holes around the conchas were punched rather than drilled; designs are stamped with repoussé work added in the center of each concha.*

Small silver canteen-shaped containers for carrying tobacco were copied from rawhide ones carried by Mexicans.

The headbands of bridles were covered with wide strips of silver that almost concealed the leather. Normally, a silver concha was added on either side, and a crescent-shaped ornament called a *naja* hung from the forehead strap. *Najas,* adapted from those used by the Spaniards, were worn on bead necklaces as well, and were often interchangeable with those on bridles.

Matthews also recorded the bead-making process which began around 1870. By this time, the smiths were apparently turning from U.S. coins to pesos for their silver; Matthews mentions that Mexican silver dollars were used to form the beads. A peso was pounded into the desired thickness; then a disk large enough to make half a bead was cut out with scissors. It was trimmed and used as a pattern for the others.

Half-circles were formed with a mold and die; the pieces were strung on a stout wire in pairs forming full circles and fastened tightly together. A mixture of borax, saliva, and silver was applied to the seams of all the beads; they were put into the fire and all soldered at one time. After cooling, the beads were blanched, filed, and polished.

LEFT: *The leather of this headstall from a Navajo bridle (c. 1900–1910) is almost covered with silver, which was common for the style of that era. Decorated with simple stampwork, it has a concha on either side and a* naja *in the center. Najas were often used interchangeably as decoration on squash blossom necklaces and bridles.*

Bead necklaces had become very popular by the 1900s. According to G. W. James in *Indians of the Painted Desert Region*, "scarcely a man or woman of any standing in the tribe does not possess a home-manufactured necklace of silver beads."

The "squash blossom" necklace was probably introduced around the turn of the century. It was not mentioned by Matthews in the 1880s, but was included in the Franciscan Fathers' Ethnologic Dictionary of 1910: "When arranged upon a string or thong, each necklace contains from fifty to sixty—the finer, smaller specimens often number as many as one hundred—beads. Usually they have a large crescent-shaped pendant in the front center, and in the lower half of the strand small silver crosses, and other flowerlike ornaments are strung after every second or third bead. Necklaces of this kind are very much prized by the Navajo and are certainly very ornamental."

The most accepted theory about the squash blossom design is that it symbolizes the Mexican pomegranate. In *A Brief*

OPPOSITE: *Early squash blossom necklaces. The brass necklace (top) is reportedly of Zuni origin. The Navajo squash blossom necklaces are, clockwise: small cast* najas *in place of blossoms, early 1900s; cast* naja *set with turquoise, 1890–1900; dimes used in place of blossoms and cast* naja *with turquoise, early 1900s; beads made from Mercury head dimes,* naja *with turquoise, 1940s; crosses instead of blossoms and cast* naja, *early 1900s.*

History of Navajo Silversmithing, Arthur Woodward wrote: "It is my contention that all of these beads were originally Spanish-American trouser and jacket ornaments. . . . [The pomegranate] has been a favorite Spanish decorative motif for centuries . . . it seems foolish to look farther afield for prototypes of this highly popular necklace element. If one were to remove these buttons or cape ornaments from the original garments and string them, the result would be a fine 'old' Navajo necklace." The ornament was quite possibly misnamed by a trader who thought it resembled a squash blossom.

The first decorations on silver were merely scratched in with a file. Later, a stronger tool was used to cut deeper lines. The technique of "punching" silver was adapted from the Mexican tooling of leather. Any sharp-pointed piece of iron was used as a tool to punch dots into the silver. The first stamps were made by cutting a piece of pipe in half to make the imprint of a semi-circle. Don Lorenzo brought steel dies, or stamps, to Hubbell Trading Post later, but many smiths still made their own.

The years from 1880 to 1900 have been called the Classic Period in Navajo jewelry. The time of learning was over, but the tourists had not yet entered the scene. There were numerous smiths on the reservation, each making the items he wished to his own satisfaction. They used curved figures and lines in their designs, and most used carved dies which they made themselves. Many new, and much-improved, tools were available, such as tongs, pliers, cold chisels, punches, awls, vices, and dies. Since the use of U.S. coins had been declared illegal and the Mexicans had stopped exportation of pesos, most of the smiths fashioned their silver ornaments from one-ounce squares of coin silver furnished by traders who ordered them from refineries.

Lena Lewis (left) and Jean Little at Inscription House Trading Post. Jewelry continues to be a symbol of wealth and prestige among the Navajos. Any public occasion calls for donning one's best, even a trip to the trading post.

Silver jewelry had become a status symbol among the Navajos, the mark of wealth and prestige. The "pawn system" allowed them to pawn their jewelry to traders in exchange for food and other necessities. The jewelry was redeemed when the owner had the money, usually from selling a rug or the wool from newly sheared sheep. In the meantime, traders often allowed the owner to borrow the jewelry for a ceremony or a fair, then return it the next day.

Southwestern tribes had used shell and turquoise beads in necklaces and earrings for centuries, and the early Navajos wore these ornaments as well as turquoise nugget earrings. The nugget necklaces so popular among the Navajos probably evolved through the years. As turquoise became more available, it gradually replaced much of the shell.

Adding turquoise to silverwork was not a common practice until around 1900. Even then, one large stone was usually set into each classically simple piece. Other stones, used to a lesser extent, included garnet, peridot, opal, coral, smoky topaz, jasper, carnelian, chalcedony, agate, malachite, and jet, to name a few. None ever enjoyed the popularity of turquoise.

In the early 1900s, the winds of change blew in with the coming of the railroad and the Fred Harvey Company, which established accommodations along the route. Tourism was introduced to Indian country, and tourists wanted silver jewelry. However, most of them neither knew nor cared anything about quality; they wanted inexpensive pieces adorned with garish designs, and shopkeepers were all too willing to please. Items made strictly for tourists began appearing: ashtrays, watch bracelets, letter openers, cigarette holders, and utensils.

Larger companies began mass-producing "Indian" jewelry; smaller shops hired both non-Indians and Indians from various tribes to machine-stamp cheap, tinny silver with designs such as lightning, clouds, arrows, Indian heads, snakes, owls, swastikas, and thunderbirds, the last merely a figment of someone's imagination. Lists of what these figures supposedly symbolized were given to tourists.

At that time, designs on authentic, handcrafted Indian jewelry were simply decorative. To quote Carl Rosnek in *Skystone and Silver:* "A great deal of nonsense was written or rumored concerning the 'meaning' of these symbols—when in fact, with few exceptions, they had none for the Indians."

Much of the tourist jewelry was made of nickel and decorated with small imitation-turquoise stones. Many of these items, sometimes referred to as "Route 66" jewelry because of the proliferation of shops selling it along that highway, were stamped "nickel silver."

Navajo bracelet typical of the poorer quality jewelry made for the tourist market and sold extensively along Route 66 during the 1930s and 40s. Designs were introduced by manufacturers to appeal to eastern visitors. The thunderbird bracelet is stamped "nickel silver."

RIGHT: *This silverwork by McKee Platero, which resembles that of the early 1900s, includes a tobacco flask, two bracelets, and three pins. It is decorated with repoussé and stamp-work, two of the earliest decorative techniques used by Navajo silversmiths.*

OPPOSITE: *The 1930s saw an increase in the use of turquoise among Navajo silversmiths. These three bracelets are typical of that era. The one in the foreground is a forerunner of the "cluster" jewelry that is still popular among Navajos today.*

By 1937, laws were passed stating that only Indian-made jewelry could be labeled as such, but circumvention became a favorite pastime. In 1940, the Japanese even went so far as to name a town "Reservation," so they could "legitimately" stamp *Reservation Made* onto manufactured jewelry.

In an effort to slow down the mass production of cheap imitation Indian jewelry made in sweatshops (as they were commonly called), the government ordered that only handmade jewelry could be sold at National Parks and Monuments, and some schools began teaching silversmithing.

However, these were troubled times and, with war looming on the horizon, the government had other concerns. In 1941 it did form the Navajo Arts and Crafts Guild to emphasize quality work and encourage the casting of silver; consequently, the skills of many artists improved. The project had to be dropped during World War II, but the Navajo Tribe was allowed to take it over.

BELOW: *The steel bracelet with stampwork (top), circa late 1870s or 80s, is an example of very early Navajo work. The silver bracelet with stamped designs (bottom) is from a later period, probably around 1920.*

Despite the problems facing the world and the degradation of their craft during the early 1900s, there were many smiths who never lessened their standards. Superb craftsmen continued to set high-grade stones in quality silver, and some excellent jewelry of that period is considered classic.

The use of turquoise had increased through the years, and a few jewelers began adopting the Zuni style of setting multiple stones close together in silver. A larger piece of turquoise was surrounded by small stones, thus forming a cluster. This "cluster style" was a change for Navajo silversmiths, but the Navajos have always accepted change—when it benefited them. Experimenting with new techniques and styles was a change they welcomed.

OPPOSITE, TOP: *Navajo Mountain, sacred to the Navajo, on the Arizona/ Utah border.*

BOTTOM: *Marco Begaye fabricated this contemporary silver and coral ensemble. The necklace design was adapted from the traditional squash blossom necklace first made by the Navajo over a century earlier.*

CHANGING
TIMES

CHANGING TIMES

The end of World War II brought more and significant changes to Navajo country. Many Navajos who had rarely left the reservation before the war had now traveled to the far reaches of the globe, courtesy of the military. Others had been residing in urban areas in order to work in defense plants. A whole new world had opened up for the Navajos. With the improvement of roads and a slightly improved economy, wagons were traded for pickup trucks. People began to travel more, and the pawn system began to falter as cash was spent off the reservation. The smiths had been using sheet silver rather than silver slugs since the 1920s, but they were now able to obtain new equipment—saws, vises, gasoline torches, and

Stephen Begay combined overlay and stamping techniques to form this striking silver jewelry. Although he uses traditional motifs, his work appears very contemporary.

motor-driven lapidary wheels with diamond-toothed saws. Since the electricity necessary to work some of this equipment was now available in less remote areas, some smiths moved to, or nearer to, off-reservation towns.

Although the trading posts began to diminish in importance at that time, most of them continued to serve the Navajos for many more years. Most of today's trading posts are little more than convenience markets, but a few, primarily in very remote areas, still retain some of the old-time flavor. The McGee family is one that has been in the trading business for generations at Piñon and Keams Canyon, Arizona.

"There has been a steady decline in trading posts," said Bruce McGee, who now operates McGee's Gallery in Holbrook. "Trading posts are almost a thing of the past. An old trader told me this story to show what brought that about. He said he told a young Navajo to give him his credit card. The Navajo looked at him for a minute, then handed him the card. The trader said, 'Okay, now tell me that you can get along without me.' Pawn was the credit card of the early days."

Joe Tanner, of Tanner's Indian Arts in Gallup, New Mexico, comes from a long line of traders. "The pawn system is still very much in effect," he said. "It's just that it has left the trading posts and moved into the nearby towns. Having pawn is like having a post office inside the store. It gets the people in. We deal in a lot of pawn, and probably no more than 2 percent ever 'goes dead' [is sold for lack of payment to redeem]. We want the people to keep coming in the store, and as long as the pawn is alive, they keep coming. I would venture to say that there are millions of dollars lent against pawn in Gallup alone."

For years, the Navajos depended on traders for more than just their physical needs; they looked to them for advice on making jewelry, rugs, pottery, baskets, and other items that would attract buyers. For that very reason, traders had a profound impact on Native American arts and crafts. They often suggested design or color changes, and they furnished most of the necessary materials. Following World War II, jewelry styles remained basically the same, and those made by certain tribes fell into specific categories. Although the Zunis learned silversmithing from the Navajos around 1872, and the Hopis in turn learned from the Zunis in the later 1800s, each tribe developed styles and skills particular to its own people. The Zunis were noted for their lapidary work—mosaic, inlay, needlepoint—as well as carved fetishes; the Hopis for overlay; and the Navajos for massive pieces, symmetrical and simple, set with large stones.

However, in the fifties, a few Native Americans led Indian jewelry in an entirely new direction. Hopi jeweler Charles Loloma was the first to use rare gems and exotic stones to create colorful collages on sculpturesque gold and silver pieces. The international recognition he earned with his bold, imaginative designs opened the door for other Native American artists, and many began to experiment with non-traditional styles, motifs, and materials.

Another renowned jeweler of that era was of Mission Indian and Mexican descent, but was raised as a Hopi. Preston Monongye's unique gold and silver creations included intricate lapidary work, and he often combined his work with that of another artist. Many of today's Navajo jewelers learned their skills under Preston's tutelage, including his son, Jesse, whose mother was Navajo.

The most noted Navajo jeweler during the late forties and early fifties was Kenneth Begay. Forgoing the massive look of Navajo silverwork, he blended graceful curved lines and simple elegance into innovative contemporary styles. At Navajo

OPPOSITE: *This bracelet and squash blossom necklace combine the talents of David Lister, silversmith, and his wife, Alice, who does the lapidary. In this unusual necklace, the squash blossoms are replaced by rectangular, oval, heart, and teardrop shapes set with spiny oyster shell, malachite, and turquoise. The bracelet contains turquoise and spiny oyster.*

BELOW: *A classic example of the massive Navajo bracelets of the 1940s. Stampwork and twisted wire designs are highlighted by a "slab" of Morenci turquoise.*

The simple elegance of jewelry by Kenneth Begay, a teacher and leader among Navajo silversmiths as early as the 1940s and 50s. Noted for introducing a new style that led away from the massive jewelry of that era, he made these pieces during the 1960s and 70s.

Community College, he taught many of today's Navajo artists and influenced even more, including his son, Harvey, and James Little.

The sixties brought an ever-increasing interest in Native American cultures, starting with the college-aged group and eventually spreading throughout the country to all ages. Headbands, fringed leather jackets, beadwork, and silver and turquoise jewelry became the rage, as Indian "wannabes" effected Native American lifestyles and philosophies. Indians were "in"!

The Indian jewelry craze of the seventies swept the country like a firestorm, and a century-old craft became an overnight sensation. It has been rumored that the *Wall Street Journal* lit the first small flame by suggesting that turquoise and silver were good investments, but there seems to be no proof that the statement ever saw print.

Regardless of who or what started the trend, it rapidly gained momentum. Hollywood stars began wearing squash blossom necklaces, concha belts, and silver bracelets, rings, and earrings. Designers draped fashion models with silver and turquoise jewelry, and buyers for upscale retail stores traveled to the Southwest to select special pieces for their clientele. In the November 1972 *New York Post*, a fashion editor wrote, "It looks as if the American Indians are ready to take back Manhattan."

Navajo cluster bracelets made by Jimmy Yellowhair during the 1970s.

Arizona Highways magazine fueled the flames by devoting the entire January 1974 issue to Indian jewelry. According to Joseph Stacey, then editor of the magazine, "Single copies eventually sold for fifty dollars, and the magazine went into an unprecedented fourth printing." A six-edition collector series followed, three devoted to other Indian arts—prehistoric pottery, modern pottery, and baskets—and three to jewelry.

Bola ties and watchbands had been made for years; now they began flooding the market. In imitation of the coin silver jewelry made in the early days,

This necklace, from the late 1960s or early 70s, replicates a style of the early 1900s. Beads are made of Mercury head dimes; silver dollars are used in place of squash blossoms.

necklaces with squash blossoms made from Mercury dimes, buffalo nickels, and other coins also became popular items among jewelers.

"Silversmiths were buying up all the old coins they could find," said Byron Hunter, Manager of The Heard Museum Shop. "Some were made earlier, but most of the squashes made of old coins showed up during the craziness of the seventies."

Manufacturers and non-Indian silversmiths again rode on the coattails of legitimate Native American jewelers, and overnight there appeared cheap, gaudy jewelry set with imitation or low-grade, treated (artificially enhanced) turquoise. Workers, both Indian and non-Indian, were hired to craft jewelry in shops. Businesses from gas stations to roadside cafes to variety stores sold silver and turquoise; the world was stocked with enough "junk jewelry" to last the entire population a lifetime.

However, there were positive results from that insane time. Impressed by the popularity of the jewelry and the prices it demanded, more Native Americans began learning the craft. Others searched for ways to improve their skills, to find unique styles, or to create something entirely new that would set them apart from the crowd.

It was a time when it became important to buyers to know the name of the person who made each piece of jewelry. Some jewelers had for years marked their work with hallmarks or initials, but it now became common practice to sign one's jewelry.

True artisans refused to join the masses of mediocre jewelers who appeared on the scene, continuing to use only the best materials and create work of the highest quality. Out of this era would come not only some superb jewelry, but some creative and innovative styles.

Tommy Singer had been making traditional Navajo jewelry since he was twenty-one, but decided he should try something different. "I opened a shop in Shiprock in 1968," Tommy explained. "I went to overlay, then chip [mosaic] inlay. As I was cutting stones one day, I noticed all these little chips, pieces of good turquoise stones left over. I tried gluing these scraps together, epoxying them, then grinding off the tops, and polishing them. I set them in the recessed areas made for inlay, and they came out real pretty. I came up with lots of different designs, and people noticed and started buying them."

Although buyers appreciated the unique beauty of the jewelry, the designs may well have been misinterpreted. Those that seemed to resemble the meaningless tepee and thunderbird designs of the forties actually are symbols of the Native American Church, a religion that combines traditional Navajo rituals and the use of peyote with Christian precepts.

The "Singer style" of jewelry became very popular during the seventies, perhaps too much so. "Too many people began copying my work," Tommy said, "and they didn't always do a good job. Buyers didn't know the difference, and I didn't like it when they thought I had made a bad piece. Some of my brothers are still doing that style but, in the eighties, I went back to traditional work."

Jake Livingston said the "jewelry boom" brought him recognition. "However, when interest dropped," he added, "I decided to try some other things. I began making custom silver-mounted show saddles, 'carving' the leather and hand engraving all the silver. Silverwork is always going to be there. Interest may go up or down, but if you're a true artist, there will always be someone who is interested. I believe in positive thinking."

The seventies had a profound impact on most Navajo jewelers in one way or another. Some of today's better silver and goldsmiths either began working during that time or raised their skills to a new level.

Al Joe had taken a jewelry-making class at Northern Arizona University, but said he "didn't do very well."

I envied people who could draw or paint, but I thought I wasn't artistic. In the seventies, I began visiting my uncle's shop, learning how to solder and overlay simple pieces. I set stones and decorated them with twisted wire. They were very crude looking, but anything sold. I opened a shop in Winslow, had silversmiths working for me for about six years. I sold the shop in the late seventies when the price of silver went so high.

I had been making anything that would sell. Then Gibson Nez told me, "Your work is nice. Why don't you stop that production work and make some good jewelry?" About that time I had a motorcycle accident, broke my leg and both wrists. I was laid up for a year, not knowing if I would ever make jewelry again. That brought a change in my life. I went back to NAU and took metal-smithing classes, and kept going to workshops.

After serving four years on the Navajo Tribal Council, Al Joe is back at the workbench full-time. He was wise enough to heed Gibson Nez's advice, and his years of study and his experiences through the seventies have made him a true artist.

A favorite story of the jewelry fever of the seventies is Victor Beck's tale of attending the Santa Fe Indian Market:

In early 1975, I went to Market for the first time. I had done some really unique designs for that show. I got there on Friday just in time to enter my jewelry. There were probably no rooms to be had, but I don't think I had the money for one anyway. I parked by the La Fonda Hotel and slept in my car. I got to bed late and slept in the next morning until about 7:45 or so. When I woke up, I looked out and there were all these people all over the place.

I went to pick up my jewelry and found out I'd won a bunch of first prize awards. I finally got to my booth about 8:30, and

Al Joe, who begain making jewelry during the 1970s, now does both traditional and contemporary styles. Both bracelets contain Blue Gem turquoise.

39

OPPOSITE: *Jewelry by Victor Beck. The necklace may be worn with the coral strands or the turquoise beads in front, or turned to show a portion of each. With added clasps, either section may also be worn separately as a choker. The four different beads on the left side of the necklace represent the Four Directions: white shell for East; turquoise for South; abalone for West; and jet for North.*

there was a big crowd there. As I started putting my jewelry out, people were looking at it, grabbing pieces to try on; some were even writing checks. I didn't know what to do. I didn't even have all my work out yet. Someone saw my dilemma and came and helped me. By the time I finally got all set up, three-quarters of my jewelry was sold. Within an hour and a half, it was all gone.

A woman came by and said, "Oh, no. I wanted something of yours." I threw both hands in the air and said, "It's all gone." She pointed to the ring on my finger and said, "How about that piece?" I'd forgotten I even had it on. I took it off and she bought it. That night I got a room at the La Fonda and just sat in a corner and counted my money again and again.

Many Navajo jewelers did find success in the seventies but, on the other hand, some excellent and very talented ones were forced out of the business. As the demand for Indian jewelry escalated, so did the cost of raw materials.

Herbert Taylor is now noted for his gold jewelry set with only the best stones, but he was one who "dropped out" in the seventies. "I quit in 1979, and didn't start again until 1984," Herbert explained. "Silver and gold had become so expensive, I thought no one would buy my jewelry. Besides, there were so many guys—Indian and non-Indian—making jewelry that the market was flooded and everyone was copying everyone else's work."

The poor quality of much of the seventies jewelry did have a detrimental effect, as did the hordes of pseudo-artists who were more impressed by the money to be made than by the craft itself. Imitation may be the sincerest form of flattery, but most Native American artists were not pleased, particularly with non-Indians who appropriated their styles and designs.

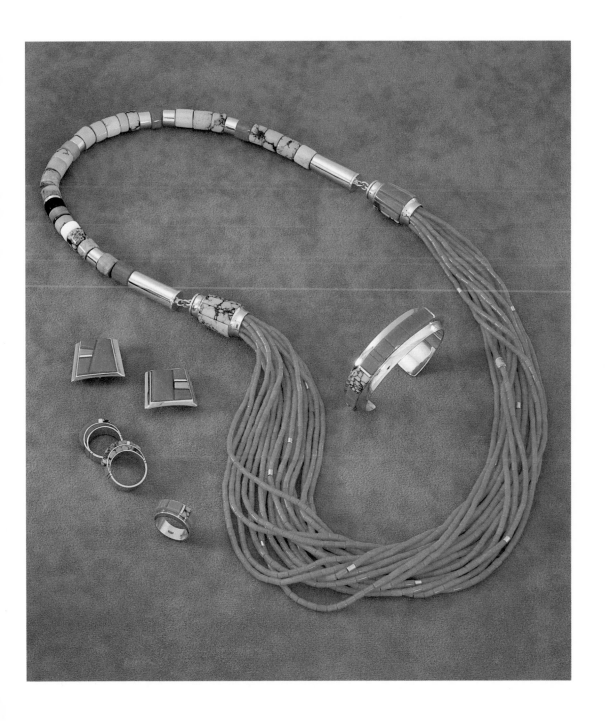

The influence of French jeweler Pierre Touraine is evident in Harvey Begay's gold jewelry set with diamonds.

However, one non-Indian artist in particular is noted for the positive influence he had on American Indian jewelry. The late Pierre Touraine, an award-winning French jeweler who lived in Scottsdale, Arizona, at the time, was intrigued by the work of Native American artists. However, rather than trying to emulate their style, he offered to work with a special few of them on a one-on-one basis in developing theirs. He not only assisted them in setting rare gemstones and refining their techniques, but encouraged them to venture into a new realm of international design.

Harvey Begay is one who is very grateful for Pierre's guidance and advice. He explained:

I thought the more I knew about techniques and materials, the better I would be. I had made a commitment to my jewelry, but I was looking for a catalyst. Then, on a trip to Chicago, I admired some rings in the window of a jewelry store and found that they were made by Pierre Touraine. After talking to him, I sold my home and shop in Colorado Springs and moved to Phoenix to be near him. He had me enroll in a diamond correspondence course. After about two months, he said "You don't need me." I began working on my own, but for the next nine months or so, I still went to Pierre with my problems. I had a lot of respect for him. Some people don't want to share their knowledge, but he sincerely wanted to help.

Pierre's contribution to Native American art did not end with his death in 1983, and was not limited to the few artists he assisted directly. Others were influenced not only by his work, but also by that of his protégés; that European touch can be seen in the jewelry of some of today's best Navajo jewelers.

The eighties saw a renaissance in Navajo jewelry. As the clamor of the seventies faded away, so did many of the non-Indian jewelers, as well as Native Americans who were not really dedicated to their craft. The market changed drastically. Competition was keen, and the economy seemed to be taking a never-ending roller-coaster ride.

"The seventies were what we like to call the 'good old days,'" Al Joe said with a grin. "Anything sold. Now the pieces have to be finer and set with quality gems. The artistic ability of jewelers has really developed, and there's lots of competition."

Lee Yazzie learned silversmithing from his parents in 1968. "I had to have something to do after I had hip surgery," Lee explained. "Through the seventies, I just kept trying to do better. After all the fuss died down, the demand was still there, but it was for quality, not quantity."

There will always be a place for tourist items and less expensive jewelry, but from the eighties on, the best market has been among those who look for quality: collectors, museums, gallery owners, and traders—all astute buyers. They understand the business and they appreciate craftsmanship and high-grade materials.

During the eighties, the work of most of the better jewelers moved into galleries and museum shops. In fact, some traders opened shops and galleries in off-reservation towns, where they continue to do business with their silversmiths in a new environment. Gallery owners found themselves replacing the trading posts in many respects. Like the old-time traders, they were expected to supply metal and stones, even advance money on jewelry to be delivered upon completion. And they not only promoted the jewelers' work, but gave advice about which styles and designs would sell well.

This is still true today and, although it is helpful to jewelers who need to create marketable work in order to earn a living, it makes some wonder if the demands of the market leave any room for artistic expression.

As Lee Yazzie said, "There are lots of things I'd like to do, but one has to consider economics. I can't devote all my time to one special piece. Bills must be paid and my family must be fed. Everything has to be taken into consideration when you're trying to make a living with your jewelry."

Harvey Begay, too, is torn by the fine line between pure artistry and marketability. "I feel that my job is exploring ways to work the metal," he said. "I enjoy metalwork, but galleries say the jewelry must have stones. Where does my personal expression come in? There must be a balance. I admire anyone who does anything different, but most of the major shows insist on traditional work. They need to expand their categories, because tradition evolves."

Tradition is at one time both ever-changing and changeless. Navajo roots go so deeply into the past that cultural mores cannot be ignored, and some vestiges of tradition will always

OPPOSITE: *Michael Kirk (Navajo/Isleta) was one who was indirectly influenced by Pierre Touraine. As an admirer of the work of the late Ted Charveze, a fellow-Isleta jeweler and protégé of Pierre Touraine, Michael added the European touch that enhances his jewelry, yet most of his designs are inspired by his maternal Pueblo ancestry. A curved feather, made by cutting and engraving 18-karat gold, forms a bracelet set with a band of Australian opal. Earrings are of sugilite and Australian opal in 14-karat gold. In the necklace, gold beads are combined with a kachina figure that has a tufacast gold tableta with cutout flute players. Stones include Mediterranean coral, lapis lazuli, opal, turquoise, and jet. The blue stone resembling turquoise in the face is gem silica.*

appear in a Navajo artist's work. Still, as times change, so do the thoughts and ideas that spring from artistic minds. If Navajo jewelry had not evolved during the last century, it would be lifeless and uninteresting today.

Fortunately, that has not happened; a broad range of jewelry styles is available in a broad range of prices. There will always be those who do traditional Navajo silverwork, but during the eighties, there was appreciable evolution.

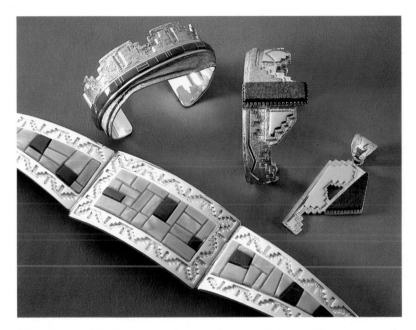

LEFT: *Gold and silver overlay by Tommy Jackson. The two bracelets are set with coral and Lander turquoise, the pendant (right) with sugilite. The ladies' belt buckle in the foreground contains pink coral and sugilite.*

The demand for better craftsmanship was followed by a resurgence of creativity and innovation. It became a time of trial for jewelers, and those who were found wanting fell by the wayside.

To create more interest in their work and to express themselves more freely, many jewelers began fashioning unique styles and designs. Some began adding precious and exotic gemstones to ultra-contemporary pieces, many of which were crafted in gold as well as silver.

A new era had begun.

OPPOSITE: *Contemporary jewelry by Julian Nez. Techniques include appliqué, stamp and chisel work, fabrication, and granulation. Nevada blue turquoise adorns the necklace and buckle at left; the bola tie is set with Kingman, the necklace (right) with lapis lazuli.*

SILVER,
STONES,
AND GOLD

OPPOSITE: *A variety of techniques were used in this jewelry. The fluted beads of the squash blossom necklace by Russ Rockbridge are fabricated; the* naja *is tufacast. The bracelets are: (upper left) overlay with stamped designs by J. Franks; (far right) stamping, texturing, and chisel work by Stacey Gishal; (upper center) appliquéed designs with a Fox turquoise setting encircled by twisted wire by Kirk Smith; (lower center) stampwork and Blue Gem turquoise by Alvin Blackgoat; (below necklace) tufacast set with Blue Gem turquoise by Wilson Begay.*

SILVER, STONES, AND GOLD

Today's jewelry artists capture the beauty they see around them and recreate it in silver and gold. Everything is fashioned from old-style cast jewelry to flatware, to silver beadwork, to the most contemporary gold and diamond pieces, to the occasional saddle and bridle decorated with silver.

Skills have been achieved through good times and bad, sadness and joy, satisfaction and disappointment—through years of growth and hard work. Success often depends on more than talent and skill; timing, dedication, persistence, and the assistance and encouragement of others all play a part.

As Victor Beck said, "There are certain people in your life that are so proud of you that it gives you energy. One time," he added, "I was doing a show and demonstration at Pima Community Center. This man was so intrigued that he kept coming back and taking pictures. He finally bought the piece I was making, and met with me that evening. He now follows my work and everything that I do. People like that make you want to do better."

While constantly striving to improve their skills, some of today's Navajo jewelers recreate old styles; others are content with tradition; still others stretch the limits of their imaginations in designing unique pieces. In order to fashion exactly what each has in mind, different techniques are used and, more often, several are combined: tufacast, fabrication, lost wax casting, stamping, repoussé, appliqué, engraving, etching, overlay, granulation, and reticulation.

The lost wax method of casting is used by only a few Navajo artists. "Most of them haven't learned to work with wax," James Little said, "especially those on the reservation.

50

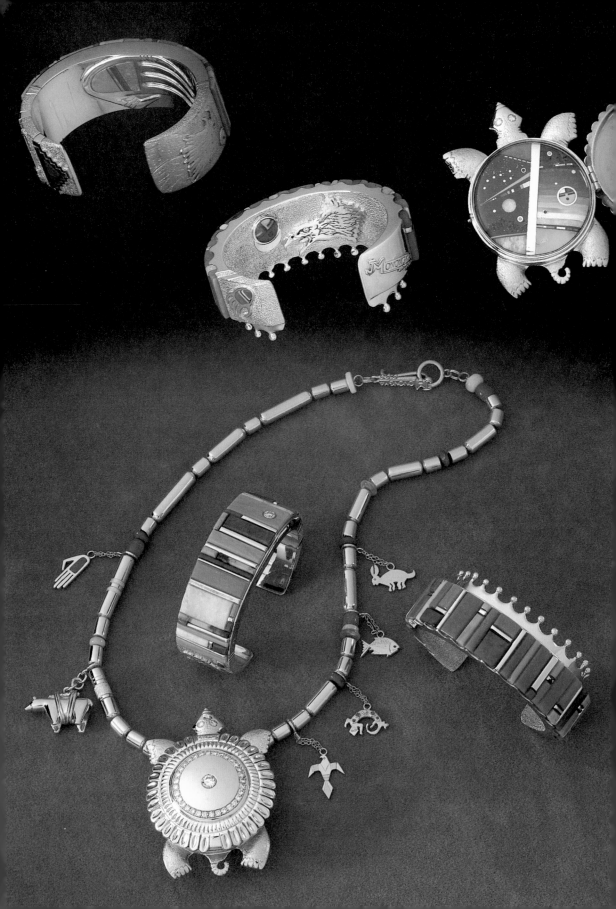

I like wax because I can make different shapes and designs that I couldn't make any other way. At first, I had a lot of problems with it, but it's getting easier."

Wax castings originate from a figure carved into wax or produced from metal, which is used to form a rubber mold. Wax is poured into the mold, creating a replica. Removed from the rubber mold, the wax replica (referred to as an injection) is sealed within a plaster-like material called the investment. As this is heated in a kiln, the melting wax escapes through a sprue, a passageway or escape route provided for that purpose. Molten gold or silver is then poured into the cavity left by the "lost wax." Although the investment is destroyed as the completed piece is removed, both the rubber mold and the original master may be used again, speeding up the jewelry-making process considerably. If reuse is not important, the original figure is carved from wax and sealed within the invest-ment, omitting creation of the rubber mold entirely.

"I did very little cast work prior to 1981," Harvey Begay said. "I didn't think I wanted to. But the more I worked, the more I realized that my highly polished pieces needed to be broken up with something different. I got interested in lost wax when I was working with Pierre Touraine and took a couple of classes. I really enjoyed it and became more knowl-edgeable about the jewelry-making process—what happens to the metal and why. Before that, I was just bending and stretch-ing it. I found that casting speeded things up considerably. Besides, wax is nice to work with because some very interest-ing shapes can be made, designs that would be very difficult, if not impossible, to fabricate."

OPPOSITE: *Made by Jesse Monongye as a tribute to Hopi jeweler Charles Loloma, the bracelet (lower right) resembles a crown—a salute to "the King of the Jewelers." Designs on the underside of bracelets also honor Laloma, the originator of this innovation. The underside of the crown bracelet (top center) reveals an eagle's head and the sun eclipsing the moon; the other bracelet (upper left), an inlaid bear paw. The pendant of the neck-lace is a gold and silver turtle adorned with dia-monds. Its shell opens to reveal a mosaic inlaid scene (upper right) repre-senting both night and day. This piece was made to honor Jesse's grand-mother, whose teachings often included stories about the turtle.*

The older tufa- or stonecast technique is still preferred by most Navajo jewelers who cast their work. Often erroneously referred to as sandcast, it is one of the earliest techniques used by Navajo smiths, and it is accomplished in much the same way it was in the early days. A design, along with air vents and a channel, is carved into a flat piece of tufa-stone, another is clamped tightly to it, and molten metal is poured through the open channel into the carved design. When it cools, the piece is removed from the mold, then cleaned, filed, ground, and polished to completion.

"Stonecasting is a pretty difficult medium," Ric Charlie said. "But to me it's second nature. Everything I do is cast, and 99 percent of them are one-of-a-kind. When I carve the stone, I undercut the design. Silver shrinks as it hardens, and it grabs onto everything. The mold is ruined when I pull out the finished piece, so a new one has to be carved each time."

"I enjoy working with tufastone," Fidel Bahe said. "I love the natural texture. You can get tufa in extra-fine, fine, medium, and hard. I like the extra-fine; the texture doesn't really look like it came from a natural stone."

One of the earliest methods used to add jewelry designs was stamping, and it is still very popular today. Dies, which are

LEFT: *The distinctive gold styling of Harvey Begay features bracelets cast by the lost wax method. One is set with Lone Mountain turquoise; the other contains pave-set diamonds.*

OPPOSITE: *A rubber mold and wax models used by Harvey Begay in the lost wax process. Some of these bracelets and earrings were carved directly from wax; others were formed by injecting melted wax into a rubber mold such as the one shown here.*

These tufacast pieces by Fidel Bahe show the natural finish of the tufastone. The buckle at top right has three elevations. The raised polished design represents a shooting star and the indented design with Royston turquoise represents a yei'ii. Turquoise in the other pieces is Chinese.

metal tools with a pattern cut or filed into one end, are used to stamp designs into silver or gold. Closely spaced, fine, uniform lines meticulously stamped into silver or gold are referred to as chiselwork.

Originally, dies or stamps were made from scraps of steel or iron, and today many jewelers still make their own. Thomas Curtis, Sr., said, "You have to make your own tools and designs to be an artist."

"I make my own stamps," Norbert Peshlakai said, "and add to them all the time. Some textures are even made with stamps; some are hammered. Others are done in the same way you would carve wood with a gouge." Nine different stamps were required to make each tiny Mimbres rabbit in one of Norbert's designs.

The stamping process was adapted from one used by the Mexicans in adding designs to leather. Early Navajo smiths transferred the technique to silver.

Stages of the tufacast artistry of Ric Charlie. Dental tools were used to carve this double mold for a two-sided belt buckle. Both pieces were blackened with a torch to form a thin layer of soot, which acted as a lubricant, and the two pieces were clamped together to form a mold. The sterling silver shot (lower left) was melted and poured into the mold (inset). The silver cooled almost immediately and the casting was removed and cleaned (upper left). The front and back of the finished piece are shown at top and upper right.

Gibson Nez actually did leatherwork prior to making jewelry. "I was like the old-time silversmiths," he explained. "I was into rodeo for years, and I did leatherwork for cowboys' chaps and that type of thing. Then I just transferred those methods to my jewelry."

Male and female punch and die sets are used to form the raised rosettes and "butterflies" for concha belts. This belt by Herbert Taylor is set with Lander turquoise.

Norbert Peshlakai's rabbit motif was adapted from an ancient pottery design. Each rabbit on the belt buckle required the use of nine different stamps. The 14-karat gold designs on the lower bracelet were appliquéed. Settings include opal (upper right) and, at far right, a mosaic of pink coral, opal, turquoise, lapis lazuli, jet, and fossilized walrus ivory.

"I learned from Wilson Jim, a traditional silversmith," Fidel Bahe said. "He told me, 'Always take care of your tools. Treat them like a woman. Be good to them and they will be good to you.' Mine are made from old files, horseshoe nails, piston rods, anything that will reharden and take a temper."

"I make all my own stamps, and most of my tools," McKee Platero said. "From the very onset I was very serious about making jewelry, and I've always hammered and drawn out silver."

Although silver wire may be purchased today, there are those who still fashion it by hand. The wire is "pulled" or drawn through a series of progressively smaller holes in a

OPPOSITE: *Noted for sil-*
verwork reminiscent of
Navajo jewelry of the
1930s and 40s, Perry
Shorty excels at stamp-
work. Shown here are just
a few of the stamps that
he makes himself, some
from cut concrete nails.
The making of one piece
of jewelry usually requires
the use of several different
stamps. These examples of
his work include two pins
(left) set with Morenci
turquoise and a bracelet
set with Blue Gem.

drawplate, a tool designed specifically for that purpose. When it reaches the desired size, the ultrafine wire is used to decorate jewelry.

Perry Shorty uses silver wire in many of his pieces, which are reminiscent of the classic jewelry of the thirties and forties. To make his work as true to the past as possible, he studied old jewelry in museums and took notice of what the older people wore at fairs and other social gatherings. Because the old-time smiths didn't have a lot of tools and materials, Perry keeps his tools to a minimum and makes most of his own stamps. He also creates raised designs by hammering the metal from the underside, a process known as repoussé.

"I don't do any castwork," Naveek said of his unique jewelry. "I feel comfortable saying that I made it all by hand. But it's amazing what techniques are out there. I like experimenting with different ones."

Naveek is noted for his channel inlay work, a technique originated by the Zunis, in which small pieces of stone are inlaid in mosaic fashion into frameworks of silver or gold. Mosaic inlay differs from channel in that in mosaic there are no silver outlines or "walls" separating the pieces of stone. In the early days, channel inlay jewelry was often a cooperative effort between a Navajo who did the silverwork and a Zuni who set the stones. Today, not only have channel and mosaic inlay techniques been mastered by some Navajo artists, but a few do the Zuni-style needlepoint and petit point as well. (Needlepoint jewelry is set with bits of turquoise or other stone that are narrow, elongated, and pointed at either end; petit point stones have one rounded end.)

The fabricated belt buckle (upper left) by Harvey Begay was inspired by a design developed by his father, Kenneth, thirty years ago (see page 34). When oxi-dized, the oval piece (top right) will become the base for a matching bola tie. Both the outer decorative piece (center right) and the inner design (bottom), which will be hammered into a dome shape, will be soldered onto the base. The small oval ring will form the bezel to hold the Indian Mountain turquoise setting.

These 14-karat gold bracelets by Naveek fea-ture channel inlay of black jade, sugilite, Aus-tralian opal, coral, and lapis lazuli. The triangu-lar designs in the gold surfaces are textured with a diamond-tipped pave graver. Influenced by both his Navajo and Greek heritages, Naveek is noted for the grace and elegance of his jewelry designs.

Fabrication is the technique of meticulously constructing or "fabricating" jewelry by hand. Pieces are cut from sheets of gold or silver, then soldered together. Most pieces of jewelry require at least a modicum of fabrication; even a cast buckle would need a fabricated bezel to hold a stone.

Richard Tsosie often fabri-cates "hollowform" or "box-style" jewelry, which appears massive and heavy, but is actually very lightweight because the pieces are hollow. He also combines overlay work with textured surfaces, accomplished by granulation, a process that involves fusing silver filings or dust onto a background with-out the use of solder. Richard is credited with being the first Native American jeweler to develop this technique. He explained:

I discovered the process as a mistake. I was filing a bracelet and some of the fil-ings stuck onto the surface. When I heated the piece, they melted.

I liked the way it came out, so I added more. The first time I entered an exhibition with these pieces, I won blue ribbons.

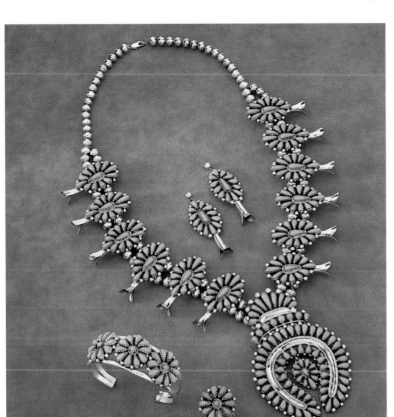

Sleeping Beauty turquoise was used in this squash blossom set made by Rose Charley. She excels at using small, multiple stones to create jewelry that resembles Zuni petit point, a style in which each stone is pointed at one end and rounded at the other.

Billy and Betty Betoney combine finely executed silverwork with needle-point turquoise (oblong stones pointed at each end), in a style adopted from the Zuni. Their distinctive work includes a clip-on "necktie" (above). Due to its even blue color and lack of matrix, the Sleeping Beauty turquoise used here is often favored among jewelers who do needlepoint, petit point, and smaller cluster work.

Richard Tsosie is noted for jewelry styles that combine overlay with heavily textured (granulated) surfaces. These unique pieces include malachite, lapis lazuli, red and pink coral, mother-of-pearl, onyx, and ironwood. The spiderweb turquoise in the buckle and on the side of the bracelet is Nevada blue; the remainder is Sleeping Beauty.

I entered an event that used to be held by Tanner & Troy's in Scottsdale, and they created a new category just for my textured work. Needless to say, I swept that category.

I had done what I started out to do, made something so unusual that people would immediately recognize it as mine. When I first started doing this in the seventies, people told me this method was called reticulation. Now they're calling it granulation.

There has been some confusion among Native American jewelers about the correct technical term for this process. Mastered by the Etruscans as early as the sixth century B.C., the European granulation technique involves fusing tiny grains

This jewelry by Lee Yazzie incorporates the techniques of granulation (the textured background), overlay, chisel work, and mosaic lapidary. The settings include Lone Mountain turquoise, jet, red and white coral, lapis lazuli, and sugilite.

of metal, one by one, onto a metal surface without the use of solder. This creates a granular texture, almost frostlike in appearance.

Patrick Smith, who has a master's degree in jewelry and metalsmithing and has studied metallurgy extensively, says that a more accurate term for the Native American technique might be "granule fusion;" Oppi Untracht in *Jewelry Concepts and Technology* refers to it as "fusion welding" as well as granulation. The Native American technique of granulation does differ from that used by Europeans, but the concept and characteristics appear to be the same. Apparently, the term granulation is applied to both.

"I was experimenting with textures at about the same time as Richard Tsosie," Lee Yazzie said. "But to give credit where credit is due, I think you'd have to say that Richard came up

OPPOSITE: *Patrick Smith's interest in and extensive study of metallurgy is evidenced by his unique jewelry. Although his work has a massive look, it is very lightweight because it is hollow inside. Patrick describes these silver bracelets as "double-concave hollowform." The one at the left is set with turquoise, coral, Australian opal, and strips of gold. The gold bracelet (right) is set with sugilite. Textured designs are added with a graving tool. The unusual surface of the earrings was accomplished by reticulation.*

with it first. I'm sure we do it in slightly different ways, because we each discovered it on our own.

"I solder my texture on," Lee explained. "I found that fusing it without solder overheated the other parts of the design. If a piece is going to be covered entirely, I guess that's okay, but I use my texture as background around the designs. It oxidizes better and gives it more depth. Some silversmiths like their texture irregular; I prefer mine even, like fine sandpaper."

"I use granulation for some textures," Al Joe said. "Others are done with a graving tool. But my insets are done with a rolling mill, using a textured plate. That might be called 'press texture.'"

Al, who continues to improve his metallurgy skills by attending seminars and workshops with international artists, said, "Too few Navajo artists take the time to really study their craft. They never get beyond cutting and soldering. They need exposure to international processes. Some of them set precious stones but don't really know all they need to know about silver techniques."

Patrick Smith uses the reticulation technique, a method used by Fabergé and other nineteenth-century jewelers from Czarist Russia. Only recently has it come into use internationally, and Patrick is quite possibly the only Native American who understands and uses this method.

"I did a lot of experimenting with reticulation," he said. "Sterling silver is added to a certain percentage of melted copper; then they are poured into an ingot mold. The piece of ingot has to be rolled back out to a usable gauge. I anneal it [reheat it to soften] and pickle it [put it in a sulfuric acid

solution] until it's frosty white. It's put through a rolling mill two or three times. I keep annealing and quenching it each time until I finally get it to the correct gauge. The fine silver comes to the surface. When it's heated with a torch, the top layer flows into free-form designs, sort of like a topo map. You can scratch a motif on the piece before you reticulate and the pattern will show through."

He also uses the Japanese process of mokume, which he refers to as a Marriage of the Metals. "Three base metals— gold, silver, and copper—are melted together," he said. "Then I roll it out, cut it in half, and put one piece on top of the other. I keep doing that until I have twelve layers. It has a really nice look. I bring color into metal by heating it with a torch. I give it a high polish, like chrome. When I put a torch to it, the colors just come.

"My hollowform pieces sometimes overpower other jewelry," he added. "I could use lost wax, but the pieces would be much heavier. I stamp the flat metal, then concave it, and finish the piece. It's hollow inside, so it simply gives the illusion of mass. It's really very light."

Robert Taylor uses the overlay technique in his "story" designs, which include ancient symbols as well as figures from Navajo culture: rug patterns, hogans, horses, sheep, weavers, mountains, perhaps even an outhouse. Each piece of his jewelry includes tiny figures cut from silver or gold. "My father was a traditional storyteller," Robert said. "Sometimes his stories would go on until early-morning hours. My ambition to learn storytelling was transferred to my jewelry. I like to try different things."

OPPOSITE: *Inlaid with Chinese turquoise and Mediterranean coral, this necklace with reversible pendant by Alvin and Lula Begay is accompanied by matching components that demonstrate both overlay and fabrication techniques. Overlay designs are created by soldering figures cut from silver (upper and lower left) onto background pieces. To add contrast, the background is oxidized and textured. Tapered rectangular beads are cut and shaped to the desired configuration, then soldered; discoidal beads are formed by soldering two domed halves together. The long lines at the top of the pendant were made with the handmade stamp directly above it, a process known as chisel work.*

Robert Taylor is noted for his gold and silver overlay "storyteller" jewelry. The concha belt, which was awarded Best of Division at the 1994 Santa Fe Indian Market, portrays Navajo rug designs, dancing flute players, sacred yei'ii figures, and four conchas with traditional lifestyle scenes. The bola ties are embellished by a flute player and a Navajo horseman. Robert's inspiration comes from his memories of the old days: herding sheep, riding horses, and watching his mother weave.

The process of overlay involves cutting a design from a flat sheet of silver or gold, then soldering it onto a solid piece of metal the same size and shape. Striking designs are created by oxidizing the recessed areas and putting a high polish on the raised surfaces. Although the overlay technique was originated in the late 1930s by Hopi silversmiths Paul Saufkie and Fred Kabotie, many Navajos today have become very skilled at this method.

"I think of my work as oil painting on silver," Charles Morris said. "I drill a hole in the center of a design, then cut it out with a saw. The fine cuts go clear through the sixteen-gauge silver; they're sometimes mistaken for laser cuts. The two pieces are soldered together, and the bottom piece is oxidized. Then I polish the top to a satin finish. I tape off the side with masking tape and sand the center section finer and finer,

Charles Morris learned the overlay technique when his father suggested he transfer his painting skills to silver. His overlay is more delicate and detailed than most and he often portrays natural scenes that include wildlife.

then tape the center and polish the whole thing. Finally, I texture it with silver dust."

Appliqué, etching, and engraving are different methods used to decorate silver or gold. Appliquéed designs are cut from silver or gold and soldered onto the piece of jewelry. Actual etching is accomplished by allowing acid to eat into a designed area, thereby etching the motif into the metal. However, few, if any, of today's Navajo artists use that technique. Any mention of etching usually refers to using a tool that resembles a graver to create texture or design.

Although some say that engraving is almost a lost art today, it is still practiced by

This bracelet with Lander Blue turquoise was probably made during the 1970s. The leaf designs and silver beads are appliquéed, individually soldered, onto the jewelry.

Julius Keyonnie used a number of techniques in making these unusual bracelets: fabrication, overlay, stamping, gemstone setting, and engraving, which is practiced by very few of today's Navajo artists. Often referred to as "hollowform" style, the bracelet at right was meticulously fabricated of silver with gold overlay that forms a hollow shank and top, thus producing a piece that appears massive and heavy, but is actually lightweight. Although there is no geologic name for the unusual stones, they are commonly called "ametrine" because they are a blend of amethyst and citrine, both a variety of quartz. The bracelet on the left is set with lapis lazuli and a 31.60-carat ametrine; the stone on the right is 30.40 carats.

few Navajo artists. Julius Keyonnie is one who excels at this method of creating designs. He first made rodeo belt buckles, which traditionally are heavily engraved. When he began fashioning other types of jewelry, he continued to include engraved motifs. He also uses a variety of other techniques in designing his pieces: fabrication, stamping, overlay, and gemstone setting.

Allen Aragon's unusual silver jewelry is set with high-fired clay with painted designs. Raised on a ranch near Chaco Canyon, New Mexico, Allen spent time as a youth wandering the countryside and admiring pottery shards he found. He first learned to make pottery; then, when his mother taught him to work silver, he blended the two skills into one unique art.

Vernon Haskie said that chemistry classes were a definite asset in working with silver and turquoise. "It interested me to know what metals are made of, and what chemical compounds make up turquoise and copper. I experimented a lot and consulted with other artists and people in the business. When you're self-taught, you learn a lot of tricks. Some things I learned were already known by other artists; some I think are special to me."

Vernon's jewelry includes both the overlay technique and shadowbox. This style, introduced in the seventies, is characterized by deep, darkened recesses either highlighted by slightly raised designs or set with stones.

"I discovered the domed shadowbox style by mistake," Peter Nelson said with a grin. "I was hammering a piece for overlay and got too much of a rise in it. But I decided I liked it, so I kept doing it."

Jesse Monongye learned jewelry making from his father, Preston, and is now noted for his incomparable inlay work. Highly polished gemstones are cut into desired shapes, some almost infinitesimal, then set into intricate mosaic designs in gold or silver. Jesse chuckled as he asked, "Do you know the best thing the white man ever did for the Indian?"

Allen Aragon's unique jewelry features settings of high-fired clay. Navajo and Pueblo designs are painted on prior to the firing process. Upon completion, the ceramic pieces are coated with a clear lead glaze and set with turquoise.

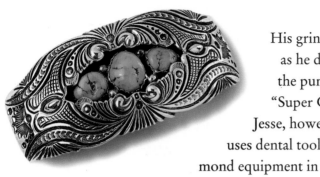

His grin widened as he delivered the punch line: "Super Glue!" Jesse, however, also uses dental tools and diamond equipment in perfecting his craft. "You have to keep working the stones to get a high-gloss finish," he said. "It doesn't matter how dull they are, there's more life to a stone than you realize. It just takes a lot of patience. It can take up to two hours to choose, polish, and shape just one stone before it can be set in place." This comes from a man who was ejected from a high school silversmithing class for being too impatient. "Finishing is everything," he said. "You need to have really smooth curves, leave not one single scratch."

Today's master jewelers pay strict attention to minute detail, as demonstrated by the flawless finish of each piece and the perfect marriage of metal and stone.

Many gemstones and other natural products are used to enhance the beauty of today's Navajo jewelry: turquoise, diamonds, lapis lazuli, coral, rubies, jet, malachite, sugilite, abalone, fossilized ivory, opal, spiny oyster shell, charoite, and others. Precious and semiprecious stones are acquired from various countries throughout the world: malachite from Africa; lapis lazuli from Afghanistan; chrysoprase and opal from Australia; charoite from Russia, and sugilite from Africa, to name a few. The use of precious and exotic stones adds an international flavor to Navajo jewelry. And silver and

LEFT: *This elaborately stamped hair clasp by A. Hosteen is an excellent example of the shadow-box style of framing gemstones. These stones are Sleeping Beauty turquoise.*

OPPOSITE: *Unusual overlay style jewelry by Peter Nelson. The design is hammered into a slightly domed shape before it is soldered to the backing. The resulting space that separates the two pieces adds a touch of the shadowbox style to the overlay.*

RIGHT: *Tom "Monk" Baldwin's jewelry exemplifies the widespread use of gemstones from around the world. Materials in his inlay work include red and pink coral, opal, sugilite, lapis lazuli, variscite, and turquoise.*

goldsmiths with exceptional talent, creative minds, and active imaginations continue to experiment with materials and designs, constantly seeking new challenges.

Herbert Taylor, who began using gold to fashion his jewelry in 1988, now uses it almost exclusively.

I alloy 24-karat gold and roll it into 14-karat and 18-karat sheets and wire. My techniques are the same ones I've always used. I still handwork and handstamp everything. I'm doing traditional work, it's just in gold instead of silver. I don't see my work as contemporary because I use no lost wax cast, no exotic stones.

Good stones are difficult to find. Many good Nevada mines closed in the seventies, but I've had some of my stones since then. Each stone has its own design; it is an art in itself. I study its shape and color, then enhance it by making the jewelry fit the stone. Stones such as Number Eight spiderweb, Lander Blue, and Indian Mountain are gems worthy of gold settings and an artist's touch.

OPPOSITE: *Materials from around the world are used in Navajo jewelry today. This collection shows a few of the more popular ones.*

Although many other gemstones are used by Native American jewelers today, turquoise remains the favorite.

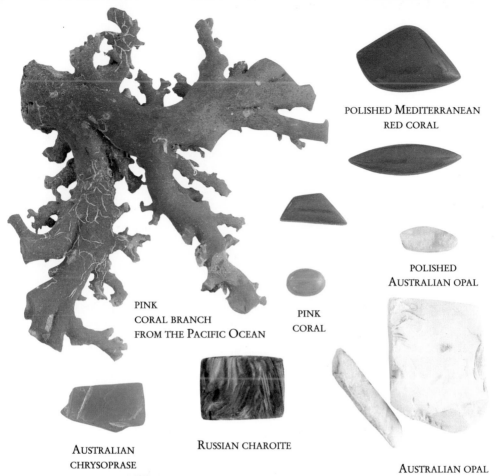

POLISHED MEDITERRANEAN
RED CORAL

POLISHED
AUSTRALIAN OPAL

PINK
CORAL BRANCH
FROM THE PACIFIC OCEAN

PINK
CORAL

AUSTRALIAN
CHRYSOPRASE

RUSSIAN CHAROITE

AUSTRALIAN OPAL

AFGHAN
LAPIS
LAZULI

AFRICAN SUGILITE

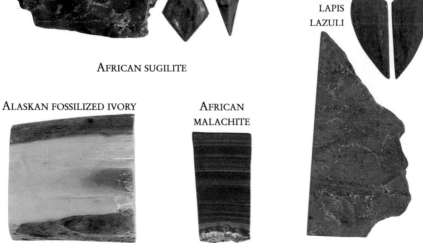

ALASKAN FOSSILIZED IVORY

AFRICAN
MALACHITE

RIGHT: *Herbert Taylor learned traditional techniques from his father and sister, but went on to produce highly contemporary work. Noted for his use of high-grade natural turquoise gemstones, he has won numerous awards for his work. The overlay technique was used to create the designs in this 18-karat gold ensemble set with coral and Indian Mountain turquoise.*

OPPOSITE: *Shown are just a few of the innumerable types of turquoise, each named for the mine, area, or country in which it is found. Any one type of turquoise may be found in varying colors, shades, and quality. To further confuse identification, more than one mine may produce turquoise with similar colors and matrix characteristics.*

It is a semiprecious stone that, simply put, is formed by surface waters percolating through rocky deposits. It often contains veins of the original matrix or host rock, and is frequently found in conjunction with copper mines. The bluer colors of turquoise come from association with copper; the greener colors from iron. In this country, turquoise with matrix is very desirable, especially the delicate "spiderweb" designs. Although it varies in color, texture, and natural design, the matrix adds contrast and enhances the beauty of the turquoise stone. There are many types of turquoise and dozens of shades and varieties of each, ranging in color from nearly white to green to deep blue.

Used throughout the world for thousands of years, turquoise has been mined and fashioned into ornaments by Southwestern Indians since before the time of Christ. To the Navajo, turquoise is a sacred stone, a gift from the gods.

LONE MOUNTAIN

LONE MOUNTAIN FOSSILIZED

EASTER BLUE

LAST CHANCE

NUMBER EIGHT

FOX

SLEEPING BEAUTY

BURNHAM

NEVADA BLUE

ROYSTON

BLUE GEM

TIMBERLINE

DANNY BOY

MORENCI

CHINESE

CHINESE

CERRILLOS

TYRONE

BISBEE

Made by Luke T. Yazzie in the 1960s, this jewelry contains some of the highest-grade turquoise from the Lone Mountain Mine of Nevada.

Their legends refer to turquoise time and again, and it is used ceremonially as well as for decorative purposes.

Turquoise has always been, and is still today, the stone of choice for most Navajo jewelers, but it is becoming more and more difficult to obtain. Most of the Southwest's turquoise mines have closed within the last thirty years due to the ever-increasing costs of bringing the stones to the surface. Not only is extensive labor involved, but there are strict state and federal mining laws that must be adhered to, and environmental concerns demand costly reclamation projects.

Gene Waddell, of Waddell Trading Company in Scottsdale, is not only co-owner of the Lone Mountain Mine in Nevada, but has been around the turquoise business most of his life; his father, B. C. Waddell, owned the Fox Turquoise Mine in the sixties. Gene said:

About the only Arizona turquoise mine that is still producing is Sleeping Beauty [near Globe]. Most of the good Nevada mines— Blue Gem, Number Eight, Lone Mountain, Royston—are all closed. Some people in the business still have stockpiles of turquoise, and they sell pieces from time to time. Some of them go around to major shows and offer really good stones to jewelers. If you keep your eyes open, once in a while you find something really special. I'm always interested in seeing any stones or old collections I hear about. It's not uncommon to buy older jewelry set with exceptional turquoise, then remove the stones and reuse them in a new piece. Finer-quality jewelry today is set with good turquoise stones, but there is a definite shortage, and this, of course, drives up prices.

"The better artists today are using quality gems," Al Joe said, "but they are getting scarce. Most of my money is tied up in coral and high-quality stones." He laughed softly as he went on. "I started making jewelry in 1972. The next year I was in a Santa Fe shop and saw a tray of turquoise about this big." He spread his hands to show a tray about fifteen inches long and eight inches wide. "I didn't really know what I was doing, but I thought the turquoise was pretty, a nice dark blue with good matrix. The guy wanted about a dollar a carat, and he gave me a break on it since I wanted the whole thing. It cost me about twelve hundred dollars. I was making these crude pieces of jewelry and setting those stones in them. I think the stones were selling the pieces. Anyway, after I'd used up about half of them, another jeweler asked where I got my stones. I told him, then asked him what kind they were. He told me they were Lander Blue." Al shook his head and grinned. "Now I know some guys that are selling Lander Blue for eighty dollars a carat."

Tony Cotner, who is involved in the operation of both the Damele and Paiute Mines in central Nevada, said, "We are getting bright yellow-green turquoise from the Damele. That's the only place in the country you find that. At Paiute, we're getting from light to very dark blue with the finest spiderweb. It's in the other half of the mountain that houses the Burnham Mine. Its just being developed, but Paiute looks promising. Every bit of stone we've pulled out has done very well. Hopefully, we'll be getting more."

Due to the shortage of American turquoise and the consequent high prices, the use of Chinese turquoise has become more prevalent. Gene Waddell said, "Chinese turquoise, like the American stone, is procured from several different mines and its quality ranges from poor to excellent; most Indian artists insist on using only the best."

"There are still some turquoise-producing mines," Joe Tanner said. "But the 'Mom-and-Pop' operations, where they would bring out a coffee can of turquoise a month, are long gone. Today, if you get one hundred pounds of turquoise, only about five pounds is naturally acceptable. Ninety percent of the turquoise today is treated [artificially enhanced]. One of the tragedies is that the public doesn't realize how much they should appreciate natural stone. One of today's greatest investment opportunities has to be in natural stones."

"There is a lot of stabilized turquoise being used today," Gene Waddell added. "And there's nothing wrong with that, if buyers are made aware of the fact that it is not natural gemstone."

Stabilized turquoise is a lower grade of the natural stone that has been treated under high pressure with clear plastic resin or other products to enhance its color and increase its durability. The treatment is permanent, and stabilized stones, which are often indiscernible except to an expert, can be beautiful. They can be found in some of the less expensive pieces, and even in some that are priced considerably higher. Some

Classic traditional pieces by Perry Shorty. The bracelets are set with (clockwise from left) Chinese turquoise, King Manassa, and (both at right) Morenci. The necklace contains Number Eight spiderweb.

stabilized turquoise is also dyed to add color, but the results are usually less than perfect, giving it an artificial appearance.

Reconstituted turquoise is made up of tiny chips that have been epoxied together and treated under high pressure. This treatment is also permanent, but reconstituted turquoise is not considered as good as stabilized.

When natural turquoise comes from the ground, it contains water which adds to its color. Even the deep, rich colors of high-grade turquoise will pale to some degree as the moisture evaporates.

To heighten the color of low-grade, near-white stones, different substances, such as oil, lacquer, polish, wax, and even water are applied by rubbing, soaking, tumbling, boiling, or baking. This temporarily treated turquoise will eventually fade, usually within a few days to a few months. Unfortunately, it lasts long enough for the unscrupulous seller to pass it off as a good stone to novice buyers.

Turquoise imitations are made of plastic, and matrix is even added. This fake turquoise is often used in "manufactured" jewelry from foreign countries.

The wisest adage to keep in mind is "you get what you pay for." A fifty-dollar piece of jewelry is not going to be a masterpiece. Beware of both dealers and silversmiths who may be less than honest. Know your source and do business only with reputable museums, dealers, and jewelers who insist on using quality silver, stones, and gold, and want to share part of their heritage, a legacy of silver and stone.

Jewelry by brothers Lee (necklace and two rings) and Raymond Yazzie (three bracelets) demonstrates the use of multiple gemstones. Several types of turquoise and different shades of coral are combined with opal, lapis lazuli, and sugilite. The green stone in the middle bracelet is Fox turquoise.

TOP: *The Totem Pole and* Yei'ii Bichai *Rocks in Monument Valley.*

BOTTOM: *Harvey Begay's contemporary styles include traditional symbolism from Navajo culture. Gold corn stalks and coral ears of corn adorn the bracelet and the pin, which is also set with a 20-point diamond. The necklace of Lone Mountain turquoise is graced by a gold yei'ii; the tubular pieces of gold on the opposite side represent the legendary First Man and First Woman.*

THE LEGACY

THE LEGACY

Navajo jewelry has been influenced by centuries of tradition and over one hundred years of craftsmanship. This legacy is handed down from generation to generation; it is rare to find a family that does not include a silversmith, and many families include more than one. Most jewelers learned their skills from parents, siblings, aunts, uncles, or grandparents.

The legacy does not merely consist of silver and stone; there is a wealth of artistic talent among the Navajo people influencing today's jewelers. Grandfathers, fathers, and uncles may be medicine men who create ceremonial sandpaintings; mothers, aunts, and grandmothers may be weavers; other family members may be silversmiths, painters, potters, basket makers, or sculptors. As children, many jewelers participated in sandpainting rituals, drew pictures, did beadwork, painted, played with clay, helped set up weaving looms, or polished and buffed silver.

Cooperation and sharing among family members is a part of the Navajo Way. Children are born *for* the father's clan, *to* the mother's in this matrilineal society, and they become members of their mother's clan. Kinship extends to both clans, and family is always the first priority. It is small wonder that large families with multiple talents pass on their skills.

Creativity and artistic talents have created better lives for many Navajo families through the years. Although jewelry making has been a part of the Navajo lifestyle for the last century, the number of jewelers increased significantly when it was discovered that making jewelry to trade or sell could provide a livelihood.

"What I've done has been good," Thomas Curtis, Sr., said, "and I have been blessed. My jewelry has taken care of me all these years, given me shelter, clothing, food, transportation, everything I want."

Charles Morris also says that his talent is a blessing. "I thank God for this gift," he said. "I learned from my mother and father who are both silversmiths; now my little sister is showing an interest. Silverwork is a tradition in our family."

Tradition is very important to most of today's jewelers. Even those who were raised in urban areas usually traveled to their ancestral homeland to visit grandparents, often spending entire summers with them. Some, who were reservation-born-and-bred, still live there today; others now live in off-reservation

Necklaces of hand-rolled beads by Cheryl Marie Yestewa, Navajo/Hopi. Reminiscent of early turquoise nugget and shell necklaces, the one at left is made of Red Mountain turquoise with spiny oyster shell accents at the end of each jacla. The remaining gold and bead necklaces are (from left to right) white coral with lapis lazuli, turquoise, and lapis lazuli.

OPPOSITE: *The blending of two cultures enhances the jewelry of Andy Lee Kirk, Navajo/Isleta. Most of the motifs were inspired by his mother's Pueblo heritage. The sugilite beads of two necklaces and the Number Eight spiderweb turquoise in the center pendant highlight these 14-karat gold pieces. Other stones include lapis lazuli, pink and red coral, opal, and jet.*

towns or urban areas in order to offer their families a more modern lifestyle and to be closer to galleries and museums. But they, too, return "home" often. There seems to be an allure about their homeland that continues to call to them.

However, even reservation life has changed. Although the pace is much slower than the chronic hustle-and-bustle of city life, many problems are the same. Some of today's jewelers must depend on other employment to supplement their art income, and even those who make jewelry full-time must also be businessmen and women. There are children to care for, school activities and business meetings to attend, art exhibitions to enter. They must wrestle with automobile repairs, leaky faucets, colds and flu, income taxes, ringing telephones, unpaid bills, and crying babies.

Yet when they sit down at the workbench, they must put all distractions aside and concentrate on their art. When calm descends, creativity begins.

Navajo jewelry today celebrates the blending of two cultures: advanced technology blends with traditional techniques; handmade tools blend with the latest equipment; contemporary styles blend with age-old designs; the gentle beauty of natural turquoise gemstones blends with the glitter and gleam of gold. The modern world and Navajo tradition are blended together into beautiful works of art.

Harvey Begay excels at blending the old and the new to create contemporary jewelry that is second to none. However, he admits that during his high school years he made jewelry in his father's Scottsdale shop as a duty. He worked his way through Arizona State University, but said that his first thought upon graduation was, "Good, I don't have to make jewelry anymore."

"There was no fire burning within when I first started out," Harvey said. "That came much later." It was after a tour of duty in Vietnam as a Navy flier, and more years spent participating in test flights at McDonnell Douglas, that he knew he wanted to return to jewelry making. "At first I was heavily influenced by my father," Harvey said. "But I knew I had to change that. For a while, I struggled to find a style that I felt comfortable with. Now I feel that my pieces are a bridge between the old and the new."

The past is always present in the hearts and minds of Navajo jewelers. James Little remembers wandering the countryside as a youth, herding sheep and discovering ancient petroglyphs and two-hundred-year-old Navajo pictographs on canyon walls. "I drew my own horses up there beside the old ones. They probably weren't very good," James said with a laugh, "but I thought they were at the time. Besides, that's the way you learn."

Navajo children usually do learn by doing. In the Begaye family, seven siblings assisted their parents, both silversmiths, with various tasks. Now several, including Vernon and Marco whose work appears in this book, are excellent silver and goldsmiths in their own right. Their years of experience are evident in the craftsmanship of their jewelry.

Richard Tsosie started out by helping his brother, Boyd, with polishing and buffing. "I didn't even want to do it at first," Richard said, "but it grows on you. One day it just happened—I wanted to design my own work."

When Vernon Haskie was five, he asked his father, a silversmith, an interesting question. "Why are you pounding on that [silver] so hard?" Vernon laughed as he explained. "He told me

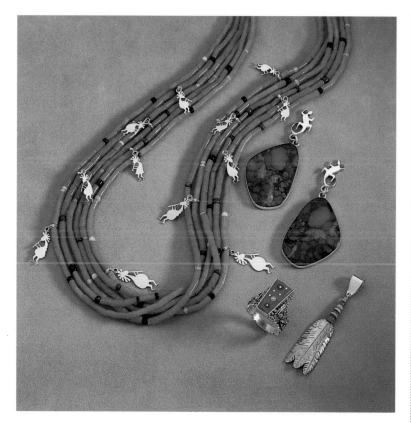

Jewelry by Boyd Tsosie includes a ring embellished with the intricate "sculpted" flower-and-leaf design for which he is noted. The necklace is of coral; the earrings are set with Tibetan Turquoise and accented by silver lizards.

he was making money. I couldn't figure out how he made money by pounding on metal. Then for Christmas, my brother and I got new Tonka trucks. I went out and pounded mine flat with a hammer. When my mother got on me about it, I told her I was trying to make money. That's when my father gave me some silver to pound. I've been pounding it ever since, and I manage to support my family."

"My grandmother was a weaver," Desireé Yellowhorse said. "I watched her work as a child. She gave me beads to play with to keep me busy—and out of her hair. Maybe that's why I still like beads."

"My grandfather was a silversmith," Thomas Curtis, Sr., said, "but he didn't want anyone to watch. I'd sneak in and look at what he was working on."

Artistic ability and creativity seem to be inherent traits among Navajos. They are extremely talented, and have always been known as an adaptable people with the ability to learn easily and rapidly. Comparatively few of today's jewelers actually attended jewelry or metallurgy classes. Many are basically self-taught, having learned the basics from books or from family members or other silversmiths, sometimes simply by observing. Whichever route they chose, they were soon on their own.

OPPOSITE: *Ten different Navajo rug styles are replicated in an award-winning silver belt by Vernon Haskie. The bola tie, which also won an award at the 1993 Gallup Intertribal Indian Ceremonial, is set with Morenci turquoise.*

LEFT: *A variety of gem-stones are used in handmade beads by Desireé Yellowhorse. She also made the center pendant; the other two pendants were made by Paul Platero.*

This gold inlay jewelry was made by Jake Livingston (two additional views of the bracelet are shown at top). The reversible pendant in the center of the bracelet rotates; one side has a sun-face design; the other, a blue jay. Settings are of turquoise, lapis lazuli, sugilite, coral, and shell. Influenced by both his Navajo and Zuni heritages, Jake combines legendary Navajo figures such as the yei'ii with delicate inlay of bird and plant life that resembles the work of his Zuni uncle, Dennis Edaakie.

"I didn't have formal classes," Vernon Haskie said. "I learned a lot by observation. I can usually 'catch on' to how something is done just by looking at it. Guess I have something of a photographic memory when it comes to art."

"Maybe some people are gifted," Jake Livingston said. "I just see something in my mind, and pretty soon it's right there on the table." Jake, who has perfected the inlay techniques of

his mother's
Zuni tribe, made
a difficult and
demanding skill sound
quite simple. "All it takes
is confidence," he said.
"You think about the person
who is going to buy the piece
you're making, then make it
good." Jake's wife, Irene, assists with
the inlay.

It is not unusual for husbands and
wives to combine their talents in fashioning
this wearable art. Perhaps this is due, at least in part, to the
spirit of family cooperation that is so prevalent in Navajo
families. At times, both women and children assist in jewelry
making but take none of the credit. There are women jewelers
today who fashion their own jewelry and, although they are
still far outnumbered in this field, they are every bit as skillful
as their male counterparts. However, collaborating on jewelry
making seems to work well for many Navajo couples.

Everett Teller does the cutting and fabricating of the pieces
he and his wife make. Mary designs them, does the lapidary,
and makes the handbraided silver straps for bolas and necklaces, each piece of which is meticulously soldered together. It
takes twenty-four to thirty hours to make the silver wire, then
two or three very long days to make one strap. "When we first
started," Mary laughed, "we bought books, then bought the
tools we saw in those books before we even knew what to do
with them."

LEFT: *Bola tie by silver-smith Everett Teller and his wife, Mary, who does the lapidary. She also performs the time-consuming task of handbraiding strands of silver wire for the straps. Inlaid stones include turquoise, pink coral, and lapis lazuli.*

Alvin and Lula Begay are another husband-and-wife team. Alvin learned his skills from Tommy Singer in 1973, and perfected them while working for Abraham Begay and Al Joe through the years. Although Lula's parents were silversmiths, and she is the niece of two noted jewelers, Tommy Singer and Betty Betoney, she didn't learn to work silver until Alvin began teaching her in 1991. Alvin now does the overall

Richard and Rita Begay work together in combining a variety of stones with scenes which often include traditional Navajo lifestyle.

design and construction of the piece; Lula cuts and sets the stones, does the final polishing and finishing, and braids the leather bola ties.

Hank and Olivia Whitethorne specialize in massive silver pieces with bold, colorful inlaid designs. Hank does the larger pieces, while Olivia usually makes the earrings. "She helps me with the feminine side of my work," Hank said with a grin.

"I just know when something won't be pleasing to a woman," Olivia agreed. "I look at it and say 'No, take that out. That doesn't work.' He cries around a lot," she added with a rather mischievous grin, "but he usually does it."

Carl and Irene Clark employ a technique referred to as "micro-fine inlay." Irene designs most of the pieces and does the metalwork; Carl meticulously grinds the stones to minute sizes that he then fits together in mosaic patterns. Carl said they "use the fine inlay as the picture, the silver or gold as the frame." To emphasize the fineness of the inlay, different colors and shades of gemstones, such as sugilite and turquoise, are intermingled.

As an expression of beauty, the color and pattern of the stones must create a sense of balance and harmony, ingredients essential to a good Navajo life.

"I instinctively choose colors that please the eye," Jesse Monongye said. "Beauty surrounds us, and all of my inlay designs convey that concept."

He continued, "A 'centered' person always starts in the middle. My grandmother was a weaver. She divided the strings on her loom into four directions, focused on the middle, and brought the corners of the design together. I begin my inlay in the center, and design the piece as I work, choosing colors as I go."

Both color and the Four Directions are significant to the Navajo Way. Colors are assigned to the parts of the sky in each of the Four Directions: East is white and, continuing sunwise, South is blue, West is yellow, and North is black.

Symbolic of the sun's journey through the heavens, all Navajo ceremonies are entered clockwise. Many artists work their designs only in that direction. Fidel Bahe explained, "In prayers, baskets, rugs, the design always goes clockwise. I

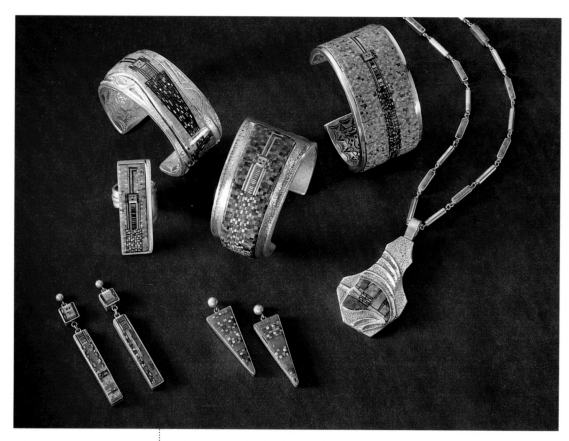

always go clockwise with my rope stamp. When I first started out, Edison Smith [a traditional jeweler] helped me quite a bit. I met him later at a show and he gave me a great critique of my work. He said 'Brother, you're doing something right. You're going clockwise.'"

Steeped in ancient tradition, today's jewelry is alive with innovation and sings with beauty. Navajo artists not only create beauty, but are surrounded by it. The world is meant to be a place of happiness, health, and harmony; to Walk in Beauty is to keep life in balance.

LEFT: *Like many Navajo jewelers, Lutricia Bedonie makes affordable jewelry of excellent quality. This silverwork is set with coral, Easter Blue turquoise (bracelet and ring) and Morenci (earrings and buckle).*

As they experience beauty, Navajos express it through ritual, song, prayer, and art. Many of today's designs, unlike the tourist-inspired arrow, thunderbird, and Indian head motifs of the forties, do have meaning. These include elements of nature, Native American symbolism, and Navajo ceremonial images.

"All Navajo art comes from our lifestyle and our spirituality," Herbert Taylor said. "It all starts there. My father is a medicine man; when he gathers herbs and other plants for healing ceremonies, he doesn't just go pull them up. He sprinkles corn pollen, gives it to the plant, and says a prayer. Then he goes on to the next one and does the same."

"Everything is sacred in our traditional religion," Hank Whitethorne said. "You can't just walk around without looking. You even have to watch everywhere you walk because you

OPPOSITE: *Carl and Irene Clark use a microfine inlay technique patterned after European master jewelers of the eighteenth and nineteenth centuries. Irene does most of the design and metalwork; Carl does the lapidary. Stones include sugilite, lapis lazuli, jet, turquoise, red and pink coral, and white shell. The prevalent motif is the Rainbow Yei'ii, a symbol of protection.*

OPPOSITE: *Silver overlay jewelry set with Chinese turquoise, shell, coral, and jet by Albert Nells.*

might step on some tiny insect or something. You have to have respect for everything."

Much is sacred to the Navajo and not only the deities, but every person, place, or thing deserves respect. The Navajo Way is simply a way of life that emphasizes cooperation, knowledge, and order, and centers around keeping a delicate balance at all times between man, nature, and spirituality. Ill health and all other misfortunes occur as a result of imbalance and disrupted harmony.

Healing and further blessings are attained by appealing to the Holy People through ritual. Ceremonies are comprised of many elements, including songs or chants, sandpaintings, and the *yei'ii bichai,* who serve as intermediaries between the deities and the Navajos. Performed by a medicine man (singer or shaman), each ritual must be executed correctly or further misfortune may befall both patient and practitioner. Spirituality and ritual are an integral part of the Navajo Way, sustaining the Diné so they may walk the Trail of Beauty in happiness and harmony.

"The Beauty Way of living is rethinking everything the old people teach about the old way," Albert Nells said. "In order to understand traditional values, we have to go back and relearn everything. The more I learn about traditional ways, the more I understand. And the more I study the old ways, the more ideas I get. Even in my dreams, I'm being directed a certain way, a way that is good for me."

"I have a lot of respect for Navajo culture," Naveek said, "and an intrinsic love of nature. I want my work to have a strong sense of harmony and hold a balance between contemporary and traditional."

Harmony is a continuing theme. Its significance is echoed in the symmetry and style that typifies Navajo jewelry, and symbolism is often included in motifs.

"My designs come from our ceremonies and Navajo legends," Hank Whitethorne said as he contemplated a recently completed bola tie. This unusual piece symbolizes the legendary figure *Yeitsoh*, a monster who set out to destroy the First People before being slain by Monster Slayer, one of the Hero Twins.

"The various colors of inlay in the monster's body are the people he ate," Hank explained. "There were some good people (the colors) and some bad (the black)." *Yeitsoh* wears a turquoise necklace, and his face includes a variety of stones. "That's because there is even good and bad in him," Hank added. "There must always be a balance. We have prayers that put everything in harmony, from east, south, west, and north. Even *Yeitsoh* has some good in him, so I added the white. The black is the evil."

Tommy Singer says he uses all old designs. "And there are so many of them," he said. "I'll never get to use them all. They are traditional designs that go with the songs, ceremonies, and prayers."

Prayer is a significant part of Navajo life. Many jewelers who live in urban areas return to the reservation for special ceremonies and to have prayers said over their jewelry. Victor Beck recalled the first time his father did so.

"I was getting ready to go the Santa Fe Indian Market," Victor explained. "I asked Dad to pray over my jewelry, so he got some charcoal and burned some cedar in the hogan. He blew the smoke and prayed over my jewelry, prayed that I

OPPOSITE: *This bola tie by Hank Whitethorne represents* Yeitsoh, *a legendary monster. Horsehair rises around a face set with black jet, symbolic of evil, and white walrus tusk ivory, symbolic of good. The moveable crescent-shaped band of stones is his necklace; rectangular sections are his body and kilt with his feet dangling below. Spiral designs on the pendant (left) represent dry desert whirlwinds; the mosaic inlay symbolizes flowers that bloom after the rain. The beaded design on the bracelet set with sugilite was adapted from those on Anasazi pottery. The earrings were made by Hank's wife, Olivia.*

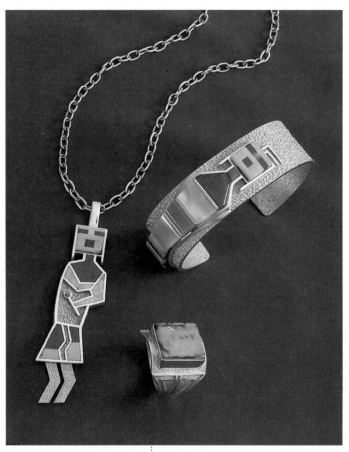

would be creative and successful, and have a good show. He was very happy that I asked him; he said he had prayed for me all my life, but never over my jewelry. That time I sold everything I had."

"My dad told me that when I sell a piece of my jewelry, a part of me goes with the person who buys it," Herbert Taylor said. "I get a mental block when my designs go with the buyer. The only way to create better designs is to have a ceremony every so often."

In Navajo ceremonies, the Holy People are petitioned to restore health and harmony, and to provide blessings. Due to their spiritual significance,

Yei'ii figures representing the Holy People are often included in Navajo jewelry designs. Here, the figures, inlaid with turquoise, coral, and lapis lazuli, complement the tufacast work of Al Nez.

the *yei'ii bichai,* who participate in ceremonies, are a prominent subject in Navajo jewelry. By inlaying them in a kaleidoscope of colors, etching them into silver, and casting them into gold, the artists offer a glimpse into Navajo spiritual life.

Both Harvey Begay and James Little, two of today's most exemplary contemporary jewelers, incorporate *yei'iis* into their work, as well as motifs symbolizing the Four Directions, First Man and First Woman, and other legendary figures.

"*Yei'iis* give a sense of power," Ric Charlie said. "They are spiritual healers and gods who protect."

Artists are inspired not only by Navajo spirituality, but by their lifestyle and cultural arts and crafts. Rug designs are often incorporated into jewelry. Some are simple motifs that symbolize some portion of a rug pattern; others are complex and intricately inlaid with colored gemstones or overlaid in silver or gold.

"I learned the perfection of my craft from weavers, their pursuit of balance and technical perfection," Jesse Monongye said. "The songs the women sang and the soothing sound of the loom stayed with me as I began working at the jeweler's bench years later."

Noted for his exceptional tufacast work (see page 57), Ric Charlie incorporates yei'ii figures and Navajo landscapes into silverwork that is enhanced by colorful patinas. The box with a hinged top is made of six cast pieces soldered together; a male and female yei'ii grace the belt buckle, which has a cast Monument Valley scene on the reverse side.

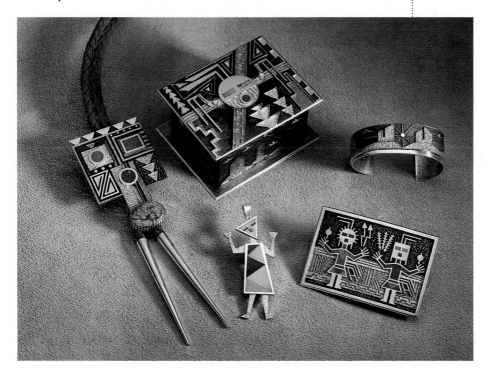

Some are inspired by memories of mothers and grand-mothers at the loom, others by their heritage, their homeland, nature, or the Beauty Way, some by art itself.

"I use any stone that appeals to me in my lapidary work," Al Nez said. "New designs sometimes come from looking at a piece I've already finished. I may use the same design, but in a different way."

Tsosie and Mary Taylor, who collaborate on their jewelry, say they get most of their ideas from simple things that they enjoy. "Anything that's going on around us," Tsosie said, "anything we're interested in. Ideas don't always come easy, but it gradually all comes together. Mary has ideas and adds them to mine."

"He is very quiet, and can sit and read for hours," Mary said. "Sometimes, when we're driving along, he won't say any-thing for the longest time. Then he suddenly starts drawing in the air."

"She thinks I've flipped out," Tsosie said with a grin.

"No," Mary said as they laughed together. "I know he has some new idea that he's trying out in his mind. People say they feel at peace with Tsosie's jewelry designs. I think that's the quietness of his personality coming through in his art."

Designs are usually more than mere decoration; they are an expression of each jeweler's spirituality and cultural identity. Certain designs are used for a variety of reasons, but most are personal and have special meaning to the artist.

Richard Tsosie includes one particular motif in most of his work. "I use the lightning arrow design over and over again," Richard said. "It's just something I came up with. The arrow is man-made; the lightning is natural: Putting the two together

OPPOSITE: Remembering his grandmother seated at the loom, Robert Henry, Jr., recreated her rug designs by inlaying them in a variety of stones. The bracelet is set with jet, turquoise, and sugilite; the bola tie with turquoise, jet, spiny oyster shell, and mother-of-pearl. In these two pieces of jewelry, 881 individ-ual stones were used, along with 846 silver strips that form the chan-nels. There are 56 small sun faces on the bola.

creates a balance. They make up the old or traditional world and the new world. The beauty of the piece represents life. There are no guarantees about tomorrow. I include the lightning arrow as a constant reminder to be thankful for everything and enjoy each day."

Thomas Curtis, Sr., who is noted for the beautiful silver boxes he creates, made his first one at the request of a client. Having previously purchased a piece of jewelry, the client then asked that a box be made to keep it in.

My grandfather had an old silver box, and the lid looked very much like a bow guard. The outline of that lid stuck in my mind, and I used that idea to develop the design of the box I made.

The ketoh [bow guard] was just an everyday thing in the old days, but we still use it today. It is our protection and good luck. It will guard us. It is worn only on the left arm, like a shield, and is used in all ceremonies. It is our testimony; the Holy People recognize us in our things [accoutrements particular to Navajo ceremonies]. The ketoh is very sacred. It is what we live by. There is a reason why we wear all our pieces of jewelry at certain places on the body. It's all part of our tradition.

Tradition is deeply instilled in most of today's Navajo jewelers and this, too, strongly influences their art. Many lived the traditional Navajo lifestyle as children—riding horseback, herding sheep, living in hogans in isolated areas.

They gazed upon rugged mountain peaks, watched skies change from cloudless blue to lightning streaked and stormy, savored the aroma of the damp earth as the storm passed on.

Rug designs decorate silver- and gold-overlay jewelry by Dan Jackson. The coral is set in the shadowbox style.

This 14-karat gold contemporary necklace by Howard Nelson is set with pink and red coral, turquoise, sugilite, opal, and jet.

BELOW: *Silver box (8 1/2" long, 5 1/2" wide, and 4 1/2" tall), set with Chinese turquoise, was made by Thomas Curtis, Sr. The design is an adaptation of those commonly used on* ketohs.

They watched the moon and stars appear in the evening sky, and viewed a virtual art gallery of sunrises and sunsets.

The Navajo way of life perpetuates a love of nature. However, nature is never taken lightly; it demands respect at all times. Believing that nature is the master of man, rather than the reverse, Navajos accept whatever it may bring, and offer prayers to keep balance and harmony between man and the natural world.

Nature speaks to and through today's artists. "There is art all around me," Vernon Haskie said. "Early morning or sunset with the evening star; the mountains; the sky; these are the things that are my inspiration for inlay. I like to use those colors in my jewelry. A painter simply creates a collage of colors in different designs. Nature does that herself; look at the rainbow."

Nature in the Navajo world does speak with an artistry of its own: in the sculptural shapes of spires and pinnacles; in the colors of multi-hued sunsets, red-walled canyons, azure skies, purple mountains on the horizon; in the textures of windswept sand dunes; in the designs of frost-laden trees, star-studded night skies, and falling snowflakes. As nature creates beauty that speaks of art, Navajo jewelers create beautiful art that speaks of nature.

"One morning when the first snow came," Jerry Begay said, "I went outside to watch the sun rise. As the sun came up, I watched how it sparkled on the snow. I knew I wanted to make some jewelry that looked like that, so I came up with a new finish."

Inspired by the night sky, Jesse Monongye creates his own interpretation of the heavens in intricate inlay designs. "I was raised with the stars and the teachings of the Navajo," Jesse said. "My grandmother always said that you don't point your finger at a shooting star. You point at it with your thumb and let it fall into your hand. If you do this right, you will be blessed and good things will happen. She also told me that the Big Dipper controls the universe. She used it like a calendar; the position of the Big Dipper is relative to the seasons. She said it is very important to our lives. If any of the stars in the

ABOVE: *The Navajo lifestyle often finds its way into jewelry designs. Here, Leonard Gene combines overlay and stampwork to blend whimsical figures with traditional motifs.*

113

RIGHT: *The necklace (left) by Abraham Begay features a Pueblo Shalako Kachina. The one at right has inlaid arrows (light-ning symbols) and a nearly-full moon pendant. Bracelets are adorned with a corn motif (left) and rug designs. Stones include sugilite, pink coral, jet, turquoise, lapis lazuli, and mother-of-pearl.*

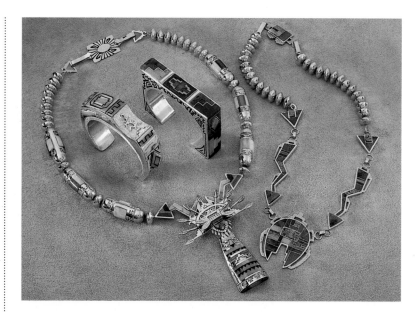

OPPOSITE: *Jerry Begay's jewelry includes represen-tations of a dragonfly (pin at right) and saguaro cactus (upper earrings). Told by his father that rainy months occur when the new moon tips down-ward so the water can run out, Jerry created "New Moon II" (lower ear-rings). The silver balls symbolize water. Early sunlight on fresh snow inspired the satin finish on the squash blossom beads. The other beads are lapis lazuli.*

Dipper disappear, it will be the end of the world. Quite often, as a boy, I would look up and check to see that they were all there. I was brought up with all this. That's why I use the night sky and the stars so much in my work."

Legends, passed down through generations of storytellers, tell of the creation of all natural things: the mountains, the sun, the stars, and all living creatures. Each was created for a reason, each serves a purpose in this world, and each means something special to today's Navajo jewelers.

"Bears were one of the four animals given to the First People," Richard Begay explained. "They were provided for protection and guidance, and to ward off evil. They embody power and wisdom.

"Corn is a gift from the Creator," he added. "It has to be planted and nurtured in order to grow; it represents life to the Navajo. I always use symbolism from my culture in my designs."

RIGHT: *The 3.96 carats of diamonds spanning this textured gold bracelet by James Little represent a rainbow. The coral, chrysoprase, and sugilite symbolize its colors. The ring is set with sugilite and a .59-carat diamond.*

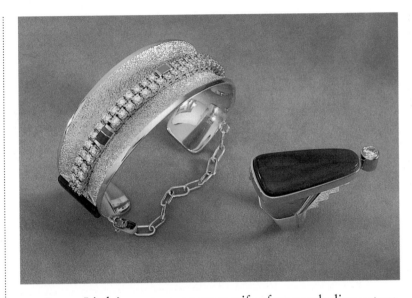

OPPOSITE, TOP: *Baby Rocks east of Kayenta, Arizona.*

BOTTOM: *The designs on this unusual squash blossom necklace ensemble by Tsosie and Mary Taylor were adapted from his mother's Crystal rug patterns.*

James Little's contemporary motifs often symbolize nature in abstract. "I don't like to just put something together in a design," he explained. "I want it to mean something. I wanted to use diamonds in a bracelet, but wanted them to have some meaning. I made a 'chain' of diamonds and, when they moved, I thought it looked like a rainbow." James attached the linked diamonds to the bracelet in such a way that they are stationary at each end but "float" loosely in the center. Even though one may not realize the significance of the diamonds, when they move on this contemporary bracelet, they flash with reflected light, becoming the rainbow James envisioned.

SHARING
THE
DREAM

SHARING THE DREAM

Envisioning beauty is merely the first step toward fashioning beautiful and wearable art. While they were mere youngsters, many of today's Navajo jewelers felt the first quiet stirrings of a dream, a dream that they might one day create beauty of their own.

Silver jewelry set with sugilite by Allison Lee. The conchas of the belt and buckle are hammered and stamped; the outer part of the buckle is cast. The bracelet and ring incorporate both overlay and granulation techniques.

However, dreams alone are not enough. Talent must be exercised, desire must be stimulated, skills must be honed, and creativity must be encouraged. Dreams are fulfilled only when the beauty is shared in designs created of silver, gemstones, and gold.

The jewelry that is fashioned today far surpasses that envisioned by youthful dreamers. The first glimpses of the promise that lay before them may have come from seeing an old bracelet in a museum, or the morning sun peeking over the mountain tops; perhaps it came in a high school art class, or while following a herd of sheep through the quiet countryside.

Robert Taylor's storyteller designs are inspired by just such childhood memories, but he would like to think that with his art he is building cross-cultural communication.

You can become a part of that cross-cultural communication with a little planning. The Navajo Reservation welcomes

tourism, and accommodations are available in several reserva-
tion communities and off-reservation towns such as Chinle,
Window Rock, Kayenta, Tuba City, Cameron, Holbrook,
Winslow, Flagstaff, Page, and Cameron in Arizona; and
Shiprock, Bloomfield, Farmington, and Gallup in New Mexico.

The Four Corners area is so large that you cannot see
everything in a single visit unless it is to be a lengthy one.
There are the Grand Canyon, Mesa Verde, Lake Powell,
Rainbow Bridge, Monument Valley, and Canyon de Chelly,
to name just a few scenic sites. See as much as possible, then
plan to return another time. You will surely want to.

Look at the land through the eyes of an artist. Drive
through Monument Valley or take a Goulding's Jeep tour to
get to places you might not otherwise reach. Gaze in awe at
sculptural shapes; imagine texture on silver when rippled sand
dunes come into view; drink in the colors that speak to the
artist's soul.

Drive down a highway and see Navajo homes and hogans
at the end of narrow dirt tracks, stop to let a herd of sheep—
trailed by a woman or a child and a couple of nondescript
dogs—amble across the road.

Notice the cloudless sky stretching toward an endless
horizon or experience a summer thunderstorm rumbling its
way across the heavens. Enjoy the fresh scent of the rain-swept
countryside after the storm passes by.

Take one of Thunderbird Tours' turquoise trucks down
into Canyon de Chelly. Sense the timelessness while visiting
ancient Anasazi ruins; admire the ancient petroglyphs pecked
into stone and the Navajo pictographs painted on towering
cliff walls; become immersed in Navajo history and remember

OPPOSITE: *This double-exposure photograph shows both sides of a seashell pendant by Vernon Begaye. Outlined in gold, it is set with turquoise, lapis lazuli, opal, sugilite, and red and pink coral. A gold fish with coral fin and turquoise eye swims across the top; the reverse side has a cloud symbol set with lapis lazuli. The bracelet, which also contains multiple stones, features an abstract* yei'ii *figure.*

Colonel Carson's men sweeping through the canyon, destroying everything as they went; admire the gnarled peach trees that bear the sweetest fruit imaginable.

Drive on across the vast reservation, past red cliffs and huge monoliths that recall legendary stories of the past, marvel at the quiet, and admire the colors streaking across a sunset sky.

Stop in at Hubbell Trading Post at Ganado, Arizona. Share the memories locked inside the stone building that still retains much of the old-time trading post flavor, and take a guided tour through the old Hubbell home.

Catch a glimpse of a lizard sunning himself on a rock, a coyote trotting across a juniper-covered hillside, an eagle or a hawk circling in the sky.

Drive to Window Rock, the capital of the Navajo Nation. Visit the Navajo Arts and Crafts Enterprises, operated by the tribe, which encourages and promotes craftsmanship, and assures high-quality products. Watch silversmiths at work there or at one of their other stores in Gallup, Cameron, or Chinle.

Stop at a rodeo or fair somewhere along the way, or visit one of the many museums or Indian arts and crafts exhibitions held in Navajo communities, off-reservation towns, and Southwestern cities. There are any number of them, including the Navajo Nation Fair and Art Exhibit in Window Rock, the Museum of Northern Arizona in Flagstaff, Pueblo Grande and The Heard Museum in Phoenix, the Millicent Rogers Museum in Taos, the Albuquerque Arts and Crafts Fair, the Gallup Intertribal Indian Ceremonial, and Santa Fe's Indian Market, the Wheelwright Museum, the Museum of Indian Arts and Cultures, and the School of American Research.

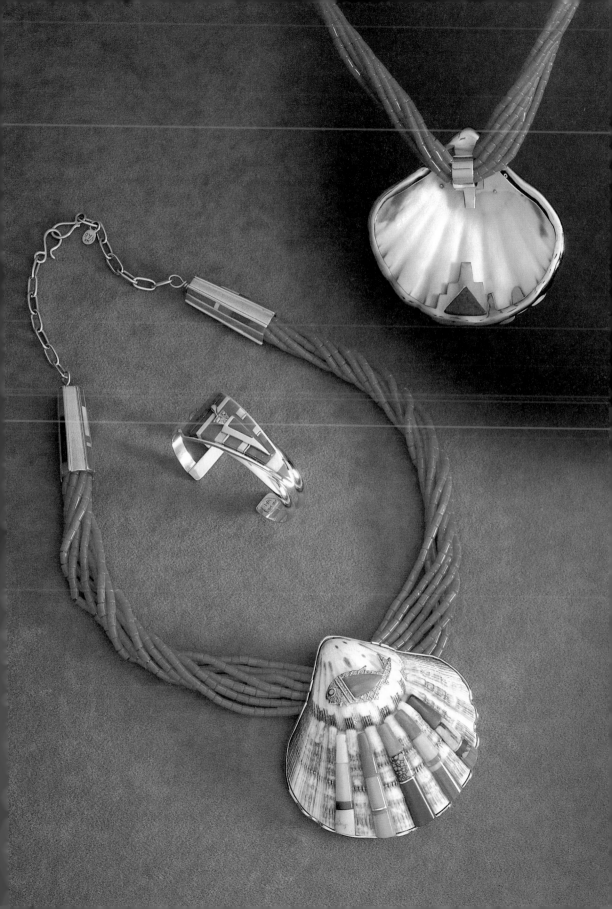

Admire the art and think of the artist who dreams of recreating the beauty around him. Share the dream by purchasing a piece of authentic Navajo jewelry.

Jewelers featured in this book were chosen for their craftsmanship and creativity. Styles range from very traditional to the most contemporary, and prices vary greatly. Each will appeal to a certain audience. Other than the examples of "Route 66" jewelry of the early 1900s, there is no imitation turquoise nor nickel silver in this publication. The jewelry shown was executed by silver and goldsmiths who use only high quality silver, stones, and gold.

However, caveat emptor cannot be ignored. Not all turquoise is gem quality, and some stones that appear genuine may not be. Not all jewelers are of the highest caliber; not all dealers are ethical. Unless you are an expert in the field of Native American jewelry, depend upon reputable museum shops, galleries, and traders to guide you in making a purchase that is perfect for you.

It is important that you not look upon Navajo jewelry as an investment, although it may well turn out to be a good one. Through the beauty and symbolism of their jewelry, Navajo silver and goldsmiths share their culture, their traditions, and their spirituality. They are sharing their dreams; look for jewelry that speaks to your soul.

Look for a special piece that you love and will treasure.

Look for the Beauty.

Share the dream.

LEFT: *Gold jewelry by James Little. The bola tie with a 14-karat gold yei'ii may be worn as shown or with the fossilized ivory feather (trimmed with gold and chrysoprase) clipped over the yei'ii. The (top) bracelet design is an arrow; the coral, lapis lazuli, and chrysoprase symbolize the colors at the base of the arrow shaft. The 2-carat diamond in the center bracelet represents a shooting star with a trail of coral, opal, and onyx. The San Francisco Peaks, sacred to the Navajo, appear in gold in the lower bracelet; diamonds represent stars, and Australian opal and coral form a trail behind a shooting star. Cast gold arrowheads, and one each of lapis lazuli, chrysoprase, and pave-set diamonds form the necklace. One ring (lower left) is set with a .49-carat diamond, the other with pave-set diamonds, opal, and lavulite.*

BIBLIOGRAPHY

Adair, John. *Navajos and Pueblo Silversmiths.* Norman: University of Oklahoma Press, 1944, reprinted 1989.

Bedinger, Margery. *Indian Silver.* Albuquerque: University of New Mexico Press, 1973.

Branson, Oscar T. *Turquoise: The Gem of the Centuries.* Santa Fe: Treasure Chest Publishing, 1975.

———. *Indian Jewelry Making, Vol. I & II.* Tucson: Treasure Chest Publications, 1977.

The Franciscan Fathers. *An Ethnologic Dictionary of the Navajo Language.* St. Michaels, Arizona: St. Michaels Press, 1910, reprinted 1968.

James, G.W. *Indians of the Painted Desert Region: Hopis, Navahoes, Wallapais, Havasupais.* Boston: Little, Brown & Company, 1904.

Kluckhohn, Clyde and Dorthea Leighton. *The Navaho.* Cambridge: Harvard University Press, 1946.

Link, Martin A., ed. *Navajo: A Century of Progress.* Window Rock, Arizona: The Navajo Tribe, 1968.

Matthews, Washington. "Navajo Silversmiths." Second Annual Report, 1880–81. Washington, D.C.: Bureau of American Ethnology, 1883.

Pogue, Joseph E. *Turquois: Memoirs of the National Academy of Sciences, Vol XII, Part II, Second Memoir, Third Memoir.* Glorieta, New Mexico: The Rio Grande Press, 1915, reprinted in 1974.

Roessel, Robert E. Jr. *Dinétah: Navajo History, Vol II.* Rough Rock, Arizona: Navajo Curriculum Center and Title IV-B Materials Development Project. Rough Rock Demonstration School, 1983.

Roessel, Ruth, ed. *Navajo Stories of the Long Walk Period.* Tsaile, Arizona: Navajo Community College Press, 1993.

Rosnek, Carl and Joseph Stacey. *Skystone and Silver.* Englewood Cliffs, New Jersey: Prentice-Hall, 1976.

Underhill, Ruth. *The Navajos.* Norman: University of Oklahoma Press, 1956.

Untracht, Oppi. *Jewelry Concepts and Technology.* Garden City, New York: Doubleday & Company, 1982.

Von Neumann, Robert. *The Design and Creation of Jewelry.* Radnor, Pennsylvania: Chilton Book Company, 1982.

Woodward, Arthur. *Navajo Silver.* Flagstaff, Arizona: Northland Press, 1971.

Wright, Barton. *Hallmarks of the Southwest.* West Chester, Pennsylvania: Schiffer Publishing, 1989.

ACKNOWLEDGMENTS

Our thanks to all those listed in the Index to the Art who furnished jewelry for this project. An extra helping of gratitude must go to the special few who participated in ways that went far "above and beyond the call of duty." Relax, gang! You can now answer your phone without fearing that it will be one of us looking for *one* final favor or asking just *one* more question. Thanks again to Alvin and Lula Begay, Harvey Begay, Jon Bonnell, Ric Charlie, Bill Faust, Byron Hunter, Bill Malone, Bruce McGee, Jesse Monongye, Perry Shorty, Joe Tanner, Eric Van Itallie, Gene Waddell, Barton Wright, and any others who may have escaped our weary minds during a "senile moment."

OPPOSITE: *Siverwork with coral settings by Thomas Jim.*

INDEX

Index to the Art

ABOUT THE AUTHOR AND PHOTOGRAPHER

Jerry and Lois Jacka are well known as a hus-band-and-wife, photographer-writer team specializing in the study of American Indians and their art and have spent some forty years living with, researching, photographing, and writing about the subject. Lois writes articles for *Arizona Highways* and other magazines and is the author of *David Johns: On the Trail of Beauty* (Snailspace Publications, 1991). Jerry's photographs have been published worldwide and have illustrated twelve books, including eight on Native American art, and four special issues of *Arizona Highways.* The couple collaborated on *Beyond Tradition: Contemporary Indian Art and Its Evolution,* winner of the Western Heritage Award for Outstanding Art Book of 1988, and *Enduring Traditions: Art of the Navajo,* the featured book at Santa Fe Indian Market 1994, both Northland books. In 1990, the video version of *Beyond Tradition,* which was co-produced by Jerry and Lois, was awarded an Emmy in the Cultural Documentary category.